Women on the Prairie

Women on the Prairie

Stories of Grit, Survival, and Unbroken Spirit on the American Frontier

By Ward McLendon

Unbound Press

Women on the Prairie: Stories of Grit, Survival, and Unbroken Spirit on the American Frontier

American Frontier Chronicles – Book 2

Ward McLendon

2025]. Practices, regulations, and technology may change; consult current sources and institutional policies.

References to real organizations, products, devices, or services are for identification only and do not imply endorsement or affiliation. Where research findings or statistics are cited, sources are provided in notes or references. Absence of a citation does not imply universal consensus.

ISBN Ebook: 978-1-971207-00-1

ISBN Paperback 978-1-971207-01-8

ISBN Hardcover 978-1-971207-02-5

American Frontier Chronicles Series

American Frontier Chronicles is a narrative history series that reveals the true stories, humanity, and depth of the people and events that have shaped the American West. Combining current research with engaging storytelling, the series goes beyond myths to examine the real lives of Indigenous communities, settlers, soldiers, reformers, and families living along the changing borders of culture and conflict.

Each volume explores a different aspect of frontier life, including spiritual movements, women's experiences, political struggles, cultural clashes, and the constant fight for survival in a rapidly changing world. The series brings nuance back to a history often reduced to stereotypes, offering readers an engaging and accessible view of how life was really lived on the frontier.

Book 1: The Ghost Dance War: A Story of Hope, Panic, and the Massacre at Wounded Knee

The Ghost Dance War examines one of the most misunderstood and consequential periods in American frontier history: the rise of the Ghost Dance movement and the tragic chain of events that culminated at Wounded Knee in 1890.

Book 2: Women on the Prairie: Stories of Grit, Survival, and Unbroken Spirit on the American Frontier

Women on the Prairie brings forward the overlooked stories of the women who built, endured, and defined the American frontier. From missionary settlements to wagon trains, from homesteads to the center of political upheaval, these women experienced the West not as legend but as daily reality.

Table of Contents

Dedication

To every woman who endured hardship, carried hope, and kept families alive in a world that demanded everything.

"What lies behind us and what lies before us are tiny matters compared to what lies within us."

—   Ralph Waldo Emerson

Preface

The history of the American frontier is often told through
its loudest moments: the battles, treaties, migrations, and
political struggles. But beneath those headline events lay a
quieter, more steadfast force: the women who supported
families, bridged cultures, endured hardships, and built
communities on land that was unpredictable, unforgiving,
and often fiercely contested.

Women on the Prairie grew from a simple question: What
did the frontier look like through the eyes of the women
who lived it?

The answer was not a single narrative, but a mosaic.

Frontier Daughters

Some of these women were settlers, some were Indigenous,
and others were migrants caught between cultures. Some
found themselves thrust into danger, while others moved
toward it deliberately. Their stories intersect with major
events like the Oregon Trail, the Texas Revolution, the
Ghost Dance movement, the expansion of homesteads and
missions, and the rise and fall of frontier towns. But they
also reveal the everyday, personal realities that history
often overlooks.

The women in this book did not all write letters or keep
diaries. For many, their experiences must be pieced
together from scattered records, oral histories, family
accounts, or the observations of others. Whenever possible,
I have relied on firsthand sources. Where the record is
silent or contradictory, as it often is, I have turned to

respected historians, archivists, tribal voices, and comparative accounts to ensure historical fidelity.

This is not a romantic portrait of frontier life. It is a human one.

The prairie was a place of beauty and possibility, but also of drought, illness, conflict, and profound uncertainty. Women carried these burdens while raising children, managing households, tending fields, facing storms, surviving loss, negotiating cultural boundaries, and keeping families alive in conditions that demanded unrelenting resilience.

This book is part of a larger effort, a series of books about the American Frontier, that aims to restore balance by highlighting the voices that shaped the West, both seen and unseen. It invites readers to view frontier history not only through the actions of the powerful but also through the resilience of those often overlooked.

Their names rarely appear in traditional histories, their labor is seldom acknowledged, and their influence has been underestimated. Their legacy is not found in monuments or acclaim, but in the families they protected, the communities they built, and the stories that endured against the odds.

It is my hope that this volume honors them with the clarity, respect, and depth they deserve.

Introduction: Women Who Built the Prairie

The American frontier is often remembered in silhouettes: cowboys trailing cattle across open grasslands, soldiers marching west, wagon trains cutting dusty paths toward Oregon or California. But this familiar picture is only half the story. The prairie was shaped just as powerfully, and often more so, by the hands, decisions, sacrifices, and resilience of women.

Women fed families from gardens carved out of sod. They delivered children in cabins built from green logs that leaked in the rain. They drove wagons, defended homesteads, buried children, documented journeys, negotiated with Native nations, and built communities where no communities had existed. Their stories are not side notes to the frontier narrative. They are the narrative.

Yet in traditional histories, women appear only briefly: a name in a diary, a footnote, a passing reference to someone's wife or daughter. The deeper truth is that the frontier demanded everything from women: physical endurance, emotional fortitude, spiritual resolve, and, in many cases, unimaginable courage.

This book restores them to the center of the story.

A Frontier of Many Worlds

The prairie was never a single place. It was a meeting ground, sometimes peaceful, often violent, where cultures collided and reshaped one another. Women lived at the heart of these encounters.

Some came west willingly, seeking opportunity, faith, or new beginnings. Narcissa Whitman believed she was spreading Christian hope along the Oregon frontier. Amelia Knight kept a steady hand over her family as disease and disaster followed the wagon train. Laura Ingalls Wilder, whose fictionalized childhood shaped American memory, lived a life far harsher and more uncertain than her books reveal.

Other women were thrust into the frontier without choice. Cynthia Ann Parker, captured as a child, became part of a Comanche family and mother to a future chief. Olive Oatman, marked by the blue ink tattooed on her chin, lived years with the Mohave before being returned to the world she no longer recognized. Sarah Winnemucca, a Northern Paiute interpreter and diplomat, spent her life navigating between federal authorities and her own people.

Still others shaped the frontier through courage in conflict, whether by carrying news across battlefields, supporting revolutionary causes, or building communities after war. Susannah Dickinson walked barefoot from the ruins of the Alamo. Clara Brown built a community where none existed. Delia Webster risked imprisonment to operate covert antislavery networks across the borderlands.

Why Their Stories Matter Today

By placing their stories side by side, we begin to see a fuller portrait of frontier life—one defined not only by conflict but also by resilience, creativity, diplomacy, and a fierce commitment to survival.

Some chapters are filled with hardship. Some reveal extraordinary leadership. Some shine a light on the brutal collisions between cultures. But together, they offer a truer, deeper understanding of what women endured— and achieved—on the prairie.

This is not a romanticized frontier. It is a real one, shaped by real women whose lives mattered.

This is their history.

Part I — Pioneers and Homesteaders: Frontier Women at the Crossroads of Conflict and Settlement

Chapter 1 — Across the Overland Trails: Women and the Great Western Migration

"Courage, my daughters. The West is yet unwon."

—Abigail Scott Duniway

Westward Bound

The land stretched endlessly before her, a sea of prairie grass rippling in the wind like waves on an ocean. Sarah Mitchell stood at the edge of what would become her family's claim—160 acres of possibility and hardship rolled into one. It was 1873, and like thousands of other women, she had just arrived in Nebraska Territory with nothing but a wagon full of belongings, a husband with dreams bigger than his experience, and a determination that would prove more valuable than either.

Sarah was just one of more than 400,000 emigrants who crossed the plains and mountains of North America in one of the largest overland migrations in world history. The Oregon Trail, California Trail, and Mormon Trail spanned thousands of miles, connecting the settled East with the uncertain promise of the West. While men often dominate the popular image of this great migration—driving oxen, scouting ahead, or negotiating with other travelers— women were just as present and vital. Their work, journals, endurance, and emotional labor made the journey possible.

We will explore what the westward trek meant for those women: the physical exhaustion, the emotional strain, the domestic burdens carried across continents, the relationships forged and tested on the trail, and the encounters with Native peoples whose homelands the emigrants crossed.

More than anything, we will examine how the trail transformed women, turning many from sheltered residents of eastern towns and farms into adaptable, resilient pioneers able to survive the harshest environments.

A Journey Few Women Were Prepared For

Most women who stepped onto the Overland Trail had never traveled more than a few miles from home. They had grown up in settled communities: small New England towns with white church steeples, Ohio farmsteads bordered by split-rail fences, and Missouri river settlements crowded with mills and trading posts. Life in these communities followed a familiar rhythm shaped by seasons, neighbors, and predictable routines.

Westward migration was almost never a choice initiated by women. It was usually a decision made by husbands, fathers, or extended families driven by economic pressure, crop failures, rising land prices in the East, or the promise of cheap, fertile acreage waiting beyond the Missouri River. Others were lured by gold in California, religious freedom in Utah, or the belief, fueled by newspapers and land agents, that a family's entire fortune could be remade on the far side of the continent.

The 1840s and 1850s were years of deep instability in the United States. Textile mills in New England closed or reduced wages as industrial centers shifted and markets contracted. Southern and border-state farmers faced declining yields from soil exhaustion, making it harder for families to sustain themselves on worn-out land. The economic depression of 1837 had wiped out savings, shuttered banks, and created a generation of men determined to rebuild their fortunes elsewhere.

Layered over these hardships was the powerful rhetoric of Manifest Destiny, which promised opportunity, abundance, and national purpose to those willing to move west. Missionary societies added their own momentum, sending families westward with the belief that they were carrying education, religion, and "civilization" into new territories.

The discovery of gold in California in 1848 added a powerful new force to the westward movement. News of James Marshall's find at Sutter's Mill spread across the country in 1849, launching the Gold Rush and drawing more than 80,000 "Forty-Niners" toward the Pacific. While most gold seekers were men traveling alone or in small companies, thousands of married men insisted on bringing their families, believing the West promised not just wealth but permanent opportunity.

For many women, the decision involved leaving established homes in Missouri, Illinois, or Indiana to follow husbands pursuing uncertain fortunes. The lure of gold transformed migration routes, increased the number of wagon trains on the Oregon and California Trails, and sped up settlement across the plains. Even families who had no plans to mine often joined the movement, convinced that booming western towns would provide better futures for their children.

An 1849 handbill from the California Gold Rush.
Public Domain.

Together, these forces pushed thousands of families toward the trails, and women found themselves uprooted not by choice, but by the sweeping economic and ideological currents of their time.

Prairie Bound

The moment they left Independence or St. Joseph, the world changed. The bustling river towns, filled with ferries, blacksmiths, merchants shouting over barrels of flour, and crowds of wagons preparing to depart, were the last reminders of the settled world women knew.

Many emigrants described a moment of stillness as they crossed the Missouri River and watched the last familiar skyline fade. Narcissa Whitman had felt it when she traveled west as a missionary in 1836, writing, "I have left the land of my birth, the home of my childhood… There is no returning."[1] For countless women, this same realization arrived the moment the wheels creaked onto the open prairie.

Once beyond the Missouri, the landscape swallowed them. The trail stretched ahead for nearly 2,000 miles of uncertainty. Women complained of blistering heat on the Kansas prairie, where wagon trains often moved in long, shimmering lines beneath a punishing sun. Amelia Stewart Knight, traveling in 1853 and pregnant for much of the journey, wrote, "I feel faint with the heat and dust. The children cry; the oxen sink in the mud. We press on."[2]

Many women found themselves walking most of the way, sometimes up to fifteen miles a day, because wagon space was reserved for tools, food supplies, and the sick. The monotony of prairie days was broken only by exhaustion, cholera outbreaks, and the nightly scramble to set up camp before darkness fell.

Weather defined the journey as much as geography. Sudden storms ripped canvas covers from wagons, flipped tents, and drenched families to the bone. Lightning was a constant terror on the open plains. One emigrant, Martha

Read, recalled in 1852 that a thunderstorm "struck down two oxen and frightened the children so that they clung to me screaming."[3] Women quickly learned to tie down everything that could blow away, including bonnets, bedding, cooking utensils, and to salvage what was left when storms carried half their supplies into ravines.

After storms, the muddy quagmires trapped wagons for hours or days. Women rolled up their skirts, waded into knee-deep muck, and pushed alongside the men because work could not wait for the ground to dry.

River crossings were often the most terrifying moments of the trail. The Kansas, Platte, Green, and Snake rivers all claimed lives. Teams of oxen panicked midstream, wagons tipped, and children slipped away in fast-moving current. In 1845, Nancy Laird watched helplessly as a wagon in her train overturned during a crossing of the Platte: "The water rushed in, and all our goods were carried off. I caught one child by the frock and dragged him up, but we lost so much."[4]

Women also cared for animals during crossings, soothing oxen, holding ropes, gathering scattered supplies, knowing that a lost animal might mean a lost home long before they reached their destination.

As the trail pushed westward, new dangers emerged. The alkaline dust of the high plains burned women's hands and faces, cracked their skin, and irritated their eyes. Water sources became scarce. One diarist wrote, "The water is white as milk and bitter. It burns the tongue."[5]

By the time emigrants reached the Rocky Mountains, the danger changed again: steep climbs, thin air, and snow that could trap a slow-moving wagon train for weeks. Women remembered sleepless nights listening to the wind howl through mountain passes, terrified that the early snows that once doomed the Donner Party might fall again. Even in good weather, the rocky paths shattered wagon wheels and tore shoes, forcing women to go barefoot, their feet bleeding into the dust.

Through it all, women held the emotional center of the wagon train. They buried children quickly when graves had to be dug before wolves arrived. They comforted families whose wagons burned or whose husbands were injured beyond recovery. And while men often scouted ahead or hunted for food, women gathered buffalo chips, cooked meals in windstorms, washed clothes in freezing rivers, and kept small children alive in an environment where one mistake, one moment of wandering, could be fatal.

Their diaries and letters show not only endurance, but transformation. As one woman wrote near the end of her journey, "I am not the same creature who left Missouri. Hardship has made me capable of more than I ever imagined."[6]

For women, these hardships existed alongside the constant work of caring for children, preparing meals, tending to the sick, and keeping families organized in a world without walls or rest.

Daily Life in a Moving World

Trail life revolved around chores, many of them more exhausting than anything women had done at home: cooking over open fires in wind strong enough to blow sparks into dry grass, washing clothes in icy rivers, and mending worn clothing and wagon covers. Yet women adapted quickly.

Diaries reveal a pattern: within weeks, eastern formal clothing was cut shorter, hems were sewn up, bonnets were reshaped, and sleeves were rolled. The prairie demanded practicality.

Illness, Injury, and Death

Illness was the most feared element of the trail. Cholera swept through wagon trains with terrifying speed, often killing within hours. Women recorded the dread of waking to the groans of neighbors already beyond saving.

Childbirth was another constant danger. Some women gave birth on the trail, in wagons or makeshift tents, then rose the next day to continue traveling. Miriam Davis Collins recalled: "A child was born in camp last night. The mother had hardly rested an hour when the wagons were again rolling."[7]

Others died in childbirth and were buried in unmarked graves beside the long road west. The sound of wheels moving away from the dead became one of the emotional burdens women carried for the rest of their lives.

"She died in the afternoon, and we buried her on the prairie. Her husband drove on with the train," recalled Lucinda Jane Saunders in 1850.[8]

Wagon Train Communities and Women's Roles

Wagon trains were temporary societies: dozens of families thrown together by circumstance, traveling for months in close proximity. Women played vital roles in keeping peace, mediating disputes, caring for unrelated children, and supporting widows whose husbands died along the trail.

When groups dissolved or reorganized, as often happened, women became the emotional anchors that helped families stay connected and safe. These trail communities were complex, but they offered women one unique advantage: the chance to redefine themselves.

Many who had never traveled, never camped, never led groups, or never spoken publicly found themselves cooking for dozens, organizing supplies, negotiating river crossings, and helping make decisions that once belonged solely to men.

Native Encounters: Women's Accounts of Trade, Help, and Cooperation

Popular myth often depicts emigrant–Native encounters as violent or hostile. Women's diaries offer a more nuanced view: many interactions involved trade, help, curiosity, and cautious cooperation. Women frequently focused on Native women: observing their clothing, cradleboards, the speed and skill with which they gathered food, and their family networks. While fear existed, curiosity and observation played a significant role in shaping women's impressions.

In 1853, Amelia Stewart Knight recorded an exchange of berries and roots with a group of Walla Walla women.[9] Knight was initially nervous, but her diary shows admiration for Native women's speed and skill as they traded and gathered food. "Some Indian women came into camp this morning with berries to sell. They soon learned how anxious we were to get them and raised their price."

In 1841, Narcissa Whitman described Nez Perce women approaching her camp to trade woven bags and moccasins for pins, needles, or cloth. She emphasized that these interactions were calm and "more like visiting neighbors than confronting strangers," though communication mostly occurred through gestures.[10]

In the Platte River region, Catherine Sager Pringle recalled Kaw and Otoe women arriving at wagon camps to trade beads, fresh melons, or roasted corn for coffee, tobacco, or cloth scraps. Her diary shows both the cultural gap and the normalcy of these interactions. She noted that Native mothers smiled at her siblings and let emigrant children touch their beadwork.[11]

Sarah Raymond Herndon, traveling in 1865, wrote of Cheyenne women who helped her party retrieve cattle that had bolted during a thunderstorm. They pointed the emigrants toward a creek bend where the animals had run for shelter; in return, the emigrants gave flour and coffee. Herndon noted how the women "laughed at our fright and showed us where the cattle had hid."[12]

Some accounts even record direct aid during moments of danger.

In 1850, Lucinda Saunders described Shoshone women guiding her party to a freshwater spring they would never have found alone, "saving us a long day of thirst and wandering."[13]

These examples illustrate what women on the trail often recorded: encounters ranged from wary to friendly, tense to helpful, but violence was rare. More often, the initial contact was economic—small exchanges, gestures of hospitality, or mutual curiosity that briefly connected two cultures.

But tensions did rise, especially as emigrant numbers grew, grazing lands were damaged, and resources became strained.

Nancy Laird wrote of Lakota riders approaching at full speed near sundown. Helen Carpenter recorded Ute men surrounding her camp and demanding tolls, something frequently encountered as they crossed Native homelands. "A band of Utes came among the wagons, asking for 'tobac' and flour. They would not leave until the captain gave them something. We were greatly alarmed, but no harm was done."

Sarah Raymond Herndon described the terror of watching Cheyenne men drive off her party's cattle. "Some of the Cheyennes drove off a number of our cattle. The men saddled their horses and gave chase, but the Indians were soon out of sight. We were frightened almost to death."[14]

Women documented both acts of kindness and conflicts, providing the most balanced modern accounts of cultural contact along the trail.

Becoming Prairie Women: Transformation on the Road

The Overland Trail was not simply a route to the West: it was a crucible. Women entered the trail as residents of towns and farms. They came out as people who had driven wagons through storms, boiled meals in blizzards, endured the deaths of loved ones, crossed deserts barefoot when shoes wore out, and slept under stars in a world without boundaries.

The trail hardened some, humbled others, and changed all of them.

By the time they reached Oregon, California, or Utah, these women were no longer the same. They were prepared, emotionally, physically, and mentally, for the challenges of frontier life.

Voices from the Prairie: Women's Diaries and Accounts

The most important sources for understanding women's experiences on the Overland Trail are their own words.

Women's diaries were rarely intended for publication. They served as personal records of private thoughts, emotional outlets, or simple logs of mileage and weather. However, because they were unscripted and truthful, they offer the most valuable insights into frontier life.

Sarah Raymond Herndon wrote in 1865, "We are getting rough and hardy. I hardly know myself."[15]

"I am learning to do many things I never thought I could," recalled Amelia Knight in 1853.[16]

These voices help us move beyond myth to discover the truth, not the polished images of Hollywood or the nostalgic stories of later decades, but the real emotional experiences of women who traveled the long westward journey with courage, fear, and determination.

Unbroken Spirit

For generations, frontier stories primarily focused on the male experiences of explorers, scouts, soldiers, farmers, and politicians. Women's accounts add complexity to that view. They show a West that relied on women for survival, stability, and community building.

Sarah Mitchell, the woman we met at the start of this chapter, remained on her Nebraska claim for 43 years. She raised seven children, survived two prairie fires, a drought, and the death of her husband in 1891. She proved up her own homestead claim in 1895, among thousands of women who filed claims in their own names. When she died in 1916, her obituary in the local paper was three paragraphs long and mentioned that she was "a pioneer" and "a good woman." It did not mention the school she helped establish, the dozens of babies she delivered, or the community she helped build from nothing. It doesn't say that she created beauty in harsh surroundings, planted flower gardens in front of sod houses, made curtains from flour sacks, and taught their children to read by candlelight.

The Overland Trail did not simply take people from one place to another. It changed who they were. And nothing shaped the identity of frontier women more than this journey across the continent.

Family on the Overland Trail, accessed via
https://www.imdb.com

[1] Narcissa Whitman, Letters of Narcissa Whitman, 1836–1847, ed. Clifford M. Drury (Portland: Oregon Historical Society, 1986), 14.
[2] Amelia Stewart Knight, Diary of 1853, in Kenneth L. Holmes, ed., Covered Wagon Women: Diaries & Letters from the Western Trails, 1840–1890, vol. 1 (Lincoln: University of Nebraska Press, 1983), 57.
[3] Martha Read, diary entry for July 29, 1852, in Holmes, Covered Wagon Women, vol. 2 (Lincoln: University of Nebraska Press, 1986), 112.
[4] Nancy K. Laird, diary entry for June 18, 1845, in Holmes, Covered Wagon Women, vol. 1, 145.
[5] Anonymous emigrant woman, diary quoted in John Mack Faragher, Women and Men on the Overland Trail (New Haven: Yale University Press, 1979), 96.
[6] Sarah Raymond Herndon, Days on the Road: Crossing the Plains in 1865 (Van Nuys, CA: Volcano Press, 1983), 72.
[7] Miriam Davis Collins, diary entry for 1852, in Covered Wagon Women: Diaries and Letters from the Western Trails, 1840–1890, vol. 2, ed. Kenneth L. Holmes (Lincoln: University of Nebraska Press, 1986), 94.
[8] Lucinda Jane Saunders, diary entry for 1850, in Lillian Schlissel, Women's Diaries of the Westward Journey (New York: Schocken Books, 1992), 76.
[9] Amelia Stewart Knight, Diary of 1853, in Covered Wagon Women: Diaries and Letters from the Western Trails, 1840–1890, vol. 1, ed. Kenneth L. Holmes (Lincoln: University of Nebraska Press, 1983), 68.
[10] Narcissa Whitman, Letters of Narcissa Whitman, 1836–1847, ed. Clifford M. Drury (Portland: Oregon Historical Society, 1986), 41–42.
[11] Catherine Sager Pringle, "Across the Plains in 1844," in Trails of the Pathfinders, ed. Oregon Pioneer Association (Portland, 1914), 211.
[12] Sarah Raymond Herndon, Days on the Road: Crossing the Plains in 1865 (Van Nuys, CA: Volcano Press, 1983), 55.
[13] Lucinda Jane Saunders diary, 1850, in Lillian Schlissel, Women's Diaries of the Westward Journey (New York: Schocken Books, 1992), 47.
[14] Sarah Raymond Herndon, Days on the Road: Crossing the Plains in 1865 (Van Nuys, CA: Volcano Press, 1983), 49.

[15] Sarah Raymond Herndon, Days on the Road: Crossing the Plains in 1865 (Volcano Press, 1983), 33.
[16] Amelia Stewart Knight, Diary of 1853, in Covered Wagon Women, vol. 1 (1983), 62.

Chapter 2 —Amelia Stewart Knight: The Diarist of the Oregon Trail

"To the West, to the wide free spaces—there hope waits."

—Oregon Trail emigrant verse

IN THE SPRING OF 1853, Boston-born Amelia Stewart Knight packed up her Jasper County, Iowa, household, gathered her children, and prepared for a journey that would stretch nearly two thousand miles across some of the most unforgiving terrain in North America. She did not set out to become a chronicler of the American West. She intended only to keep a diary for her own sake so she could "remember the little things," she wrote.

Those "little things" became one of the most vivid, practical, and honest accounts of daily life on the Oregon Trail.[1]

Across the Plains

On April 9, 1853, Amelia Stewart Knight stood on the Iowa prairie with her husband, Joel, and their seven children, staring west toward Oregon Territory. She was thirty-six years old and three months pregnant with her eighth child. Other than a brief mention in her first entry, she would not speak of it again. But it was there, present in every line she wrote about being too sick to cook, too weary to stand, too exhausted to do anything but lie in the wagon while the children prepared their own supper.

"I left Iowa for Oregon by wagon train in 1853 with my husband and seven children, and another on the way— this is the diary of our five months' journey, by me, Amelia Knight."

Their destination was the Willamette Valley in Oregon, which held the promise of fertile farmland, a fresh start, and better opportunities for the growing Knight family. But the decision wasn't made out of romance. Amelia's diary clearly shows that she knew hardship lay ahead.

Amelia Knight — A Diary of Endurance

Her diary was never intended for publication or posterity, but as her personal record. The entries are spare, factual, written in a wagon by lamplight or on the ground beside a campfire. There is no decoration in her words, no sentiment. Just the weather, the miles traveled, the condition of the stock, and the endless work of keeping seven children alive on a trail that killed people every day.

The Early Miles

The journey began badly. Within a week, the spring rains turned the prairie into mud. The wagons bogged down. One of their oxen went missing; the boys spent a full day searching for it. The tents blew down in a storm so fierce that it capsized other wagons in their company. Amelia wrote on April 16: "Made our beds down in the tent in the wet and mud. Bedclothes nearly spoiled. Cold and cloudy this morning, and everybody out of humor. Seneca is half sick. Plutarch has broke his saddle girth. Husband is scolding and hurrying all hands (and the cook), and Almira says she wished she was home and I say ditto. 'Home Sweet Home.'"

That single line—"Almira says she wished she was home and I say ditto"—carries more weight than any dramatic declaration. Seven days into a journey that would take five months, the family already longed for what they had left behind.

But they pushed forward. There was no turning back.

Map of United States and Western Territories
Settlement of the Trans-Missouri West, 1835-1860

The River Crossings

The rivers were the first real danger. On May 6, they passed a wagon train heading back east. The leader had drowned days earlier in the Elkhorn River while trying to get cattle across. His wife lay sick in their wagon, and the children wept for a father who was gone. Amelia watched them pass with "sadness and pity," knowing she and her family might face the same fate at the next crossing.

Two days later, they reached the Elkhorn themselves. Three hundred wagons crowded both banks.

Amelia described what happened next: "There is not ferry here and the men will have to make one out of the tightest wagon-bed...Everything must now be hauled out of the wagons head over heels (and he who knows where to find anything will be a smart fellow), then the wagons must be all taken to pieces, and then by means of a strong rope stretched across the river, with a tight wagon-bed attached to the middle of it, the rope must be long enough to pull from one side to the other, with men on each side of the river to pull it. In this way, we have to cross everything a little at a time. Women and children last, and then swim the cattle and horses."

Three horses and several cattle drowned that day. But the Knights made it across. They reassembled their wagons on the far bank and kept moving.

Confrontation on the Trail

By late May, the trail had become crowded with emigrants. On May 31, Amelia recorded a confrontation that nearly turned violent. Two large cattle drives were ahead of them, about fifty wagons in all, moving slowly and kicking up choking dust. The Knights had a choice: stay behind in the dust or try to pass. They chose to pass.

The cattle drovers did not take it well. Amelia wrote: "It was no fool of a job to be mixed up with several hundred head of cattle, and only one road to travel in, and the drovers threatened to drive their cattle over you if you attempted to pass them. They even took out their pistols."

Joel Knight saw what was happening. He called to his sons: "Boys, follow me." Then he drove their wagon entirely off the road, into the open country, and their cattle "seemed to understand it all, for they went into the trot most of the way." The rest of the family followed. They passed the drovers and their herds, refusing to give up their lead even when the cattle caught up again at the dinner stop.

No shots were fired. But the moment reveals the tension on the trail, with hundreds of people packed onto a single route, competing for grass, water, and the best camping spots—all exhausted and frightened.

The Real Work of the Trail

While men drove wagons and hunted for game, women like Amelia did nearly everything else.

She boiled drinking water, baked bread in dutch ovens over open fires, washed clothes in muddy rivers, soothed fevers, mended torn boots, tended to the oxen when needed, and kept the children entertained during endless days of walking.

Her diary entries were short and unpolished. They were also remarkably revealing:

"Baked bread today, did some washing."

"Children all well this morning."

"Wind blew hard all night. Did not sleep much."[2]

These fragments weren't meant for publication. Yet they have become some of the most complete records we have of frontier womanhood. Amelia captured what men rarely wrote: the emotional and domestic heart of westward migration.

The Dead Cattle and Desert Crossings

By late June, they had reached the most desolate part of the journey. Amelia wrote on June 11: "We crossed this afternoon over the roughest and most desolate piece of ground that was ever made (called by some Devil's Crater.) (Not a drop of water, nor a spear of grass to be seen, nothing but barren hills, bare and broken rock, sand and dust)."

The road was lined with dead cattle, and the smell was overwhelming. At one point, Amelia wrote that she had to wash dust out of her eyes before she could see well enough to cook supper. On July 25, one of their calves died before breakfast. Soon after, one of their best cows died suddenly, likely poisoned by bad water or weeds. They left her body for the wolves and kept moving.

The heat was brutal. On May 31, Amelia noted the temperature inside her wagon had reached 98 degrees at noon. There was no escape from it.

Illness, Anxiety, and the Burden of Care

The Oregon Trail was brutal on families. Cholera, dysentery, measles, and fevers swept through wagon trains, often killing children first. Accidents were heartbreakingly frequent—falling under wagon wheels, snakebites, drownings.

Throughout it all, Amelia's main concern was her children: Plutarch, Seneca, Frances, Jefferson, Lucy, Almira, and the youngest, Chatfield, who was two years old. They appear in nearly every entry—getting sick, getting lost, getting hurt.

Some days, she wrote only a single line: "Sick today, very weak." Other days, she described how she walked miles while carrying the youngest, her skirts heavy with dust, her shoes nearly worn through. And day by day, she felt herself growing heavier with pregnancy.

Still, her tone rarely turned to despair. Even in difficulty, she wrote: "We are all well and thankful for it."

This blend of hardship and steady gratitude would become her hallmark.

The Children

On July 22, Chatfield nearly died.

The family had just crossed the Snake River by ferry and was preparing to start the day's journey. Amelia wrote: "After breakfast, my boy Chat just escaped being run over.

As we readied to start, he came around the forward wheel to climb into the wagon; just then the cattle started, and he fell underneath. Somehow he kept away from the rolling wheels and survived with only a scare. I never was so frightened."

The matter-of-fact tone can't hide the terror. If Chatfield had been a little closer, or if the wheels had turned just a bit differently, he would have been crushed instantly. Many children lost their lives this way on the trail.

Two weeks later, on August 8, it was Lucy who provided a scare.

The family had filled their water cans at a river crossing and then set out on a twenty-two-mile stretch with no water. Lucy had been sitting on the riverbank, watching other wagons cross. No one noticed when she didn't climb back into their wagon. It was only after they stopped, several hours later, that they realized Lucy was not with them.

"Monday. August 8. Today a 22 mile drive with no water. We filled our cans full this morning, before we left, unknowingly, our Lucy behind, and not a soul missed her. She was sitting on the river bank watching the other wagons cross and did not see us go. I supposed she was with Francis in Mr. Carl's wagon and he supposed she was with me as she often came for me to comb her hair. When we stopped to rest the cattle, another wagon train drove up behind us, and Lucy was with them, terribly frightened—and then we realized what had happened."

Amelia's words are restrained: "Not a soul missed her." But the horror is clear. A child, alone on the prairie, watching her family disappear into the distance. It could have ended very differently.

The Final Mountains

By September, they were in the Cascade Mountains, nearing their destination. The terrain was brutal.

On September 8, Amelia described the road: "Traveled fourteen miles the worst road ever made, up and down, so steep, over rough and rocky hills through mud holes, twisting and winding around stumps and logs and fallen trees. Now on the end of a log, now over a tree root, now bounce down in a mud hole."

The next day, they crossed the Sandy River four times and saw abandoned wagons, yokes, chains, and the bodies of dead horses, mules, oxen, and cows lying all along the road. The mountains had broken them.

"Friday. September 9. Came eight and a half miles over corduroy roads through swamps, over rocks and hummocks. Crossed the Sandy River four times. No end to the wagons, buggies, yokes and chains lying all along this road. We passed some splendid good wagons just left standing, and many horses, mules, oxen and cows lying dead in these mountains."

But the Knights kept going. By September 13, they had reached the first farms. Amelia noted the prices: hay at $1.50 per hundred pounds, butter at a dollar, eggs a dollar a dozen, onions four to five dollars a bushel. "Too dear for poor folks," she wrote, but they bought some small turnips at twenty-five cents a dozen.

On September 17, they made their final camp near Milwaukie, Oregon Territory. It was raining. Amelia wrote: "It is drizzling and the weather looks dark and gloomy. Here we are in Oregon, making our camp in an ugly bottom, with no home, except our wagons and tent."

Oregon Territory

Journey's End

Amelia's final diary entries are brief. They had done what thousands tried but not all completed: they survived.

The next day, by the side of the road, she gave birth to her eighth child, Adam.

"Four days in camp, another six mile drive, then outside Troutdale, my eighth child was born. After this we crossed the Columbia River. It took three days on skiff, canoes and flatboat."

Amelia's diary then ends abruptly—once the danger passed, she seems to have set her journal aside and returned to the ordinary business of motherhood, farming, and settling into a new community.

She had traveled two thousand miles, pregnant the entire way, through storms and deserts and mountains, across rivers that drowned people daily, past dead cattle and abandoned wagons, through mud and dust and heat. She had kept seven children alive. She had cooked and washed and mended clothes and stood watch over sick stock. She had been terrified when Chatfield fell under the wagon. She had felt the hollow fear when Lucy was lost. She had endured Joel's scolding and the children's complaints and the endless, grinding work of simply staying alive.

And then, at the end of it all, she gave birth to her eighth child, ferried her family and newborn across the Columbia River, and arrived at a small log cabin that Joel had traded two yoke of oxen for a section of land with half an acre planted for potatoes. Now the work of setting up her homestead was just beginning.

A Woman's Leadership

Although Joel was the official head of the family, Amelia's diary makes it clear that she was the one who kept the Knight wagon moving day after day. Tracking provisions with a precision born of necessity—counting pounds of flour, tallying dwindling rice and beans, dividing the remaining sugar, and measuring out coffee one small scoop at a time. When the family's bacon spoiled in the July heat, Amelia reorganized meals and ration schedules so the children would not go hungry. Her entries reveal a constant mental arithmetic: what to cook, what to save, what could be spared.

When the children fell ill with fevers or stomach problems, it was Amelia who became the family doctor, using remedies she had brought from Iowa, such as castor oil, peppermint, laudanum, and simple poultices. She often treated other emigrants' children too. In one entry, she calmly notes that she spent the morning "doctoring" a neighbor's baby while also preparing breakfast for her own family. The wagon train ran smoothly because women like Amelia kept dozens of small crises in check.

There were many days when Joel stayed behind to help fix a broken wagon or tend to an injured emigrant. On those days, Amelia walked ahead with the children and pulled the family team herself, following the trail ruts through miles of dust and tall prairie grass. She never called these moments heroic; they were simply necessary. But her steady leadership shows that the "head of the family" was sometimes the one holding the reins, not the one fixing a wheel.

Amelia also managed the social negotiations that made wagon-train life possible. She bargained for milk, traded sewing work for fresh vegetables, and once "made terms" with a neighboring family about sharing grazing land for the night. On another occasion, when tempers flared over a disagreement about the order of travel, she stepped in to calm the women of the group, preventing a dispute from splitting the train. These small acts of diplomacy rarely appear in official histories, but they determined whether dozens of people traveled cooperatively—or miserably.

Her quiet competence reflects a truth often obscured in frontier accounts: women were the stabilizing force of most wagon trains.

There is nothing romantic about Amelia Knight's story. She did not write about the beauty of the prairie or the glory of manifest destiny. She wrote about mud and dust, sick children and dead cattle, fear and exhaustion. Her diary is a record of endurance: the daily, grinding work of surviving something that killed many people who tried it.

She was not unique. Thousands of women made the same journey, facing the same dangers, doing the same work. Most of them did not keep diaries. Their stories are lost. But Amelia wrote hers down, line by line, day by day, in spare, unadorned prose that tells the truth about what it cost to cross a continent in 1853.

Unlike many frontier stories shaped by drama or tragedy, Amelia's stands out because it is overwhelmingly domestic. Her concerns were those of managing the thousand tiny tasks that determined a family's survival. Her diary reads like the inside of a mother's mind—steady, focused, practical.

Legacy of a Prairie Mother

Amelia Stewart Knight never sought fame. Her diary was published only after her death, discovered and preserved by descendants who understood its value. Today, it remains one of the most intimate firsthand accounts from any woman on the Oregon Trail.

Her legacy is not dramatic in the way some frontier stories are. She was not a martyr, a captive, or a rebel. Her power lies in the daily labor that held her family together and in the quiet courage she showed each time she set foot on the trail again the next morning.

Amelia represents the millions of women who built the frontier not with gunpowder or grand gestures, but with endurance, practicality, and love: for their families, their futures, and the fragile promise of the West.

Amelia Stewart Knight

[1] Amelia Stewart Knight, "Diary of 1853," in Covered Wagon Women: Diaries and Letters from the Western Trails, 1840–1890, vol. 1, ed. Kenneth L. Holmes (Lincoln: University of Nebraska Press, 1983), 25–27.

[2] Amelia Stewart Knight, Diary of 1853, in Covered Wagon Women, vol. 1, ed. Kenneth L. Holmes (Lincoln: University of Nebraska Press, 1983), 31.

Chapter 3—Narcissa Whitman: Missionary, Trailblazer, Martyr

"Anybody can love the mountains, but it takes a soul to love the prairie."

— Willa Cather

IN THE SPRING OF 1836, Narcissa Prentiss Whitman stepped onto the frontier of America with a conviction so strong it overshadowed danger, exhaustion, and the warnings from almost everyone who cared about her. She was twenty-seven, bright, devout, and determined, and believed she was chosen for a divine purpose: to spread Christianity to the Native nations of the Pacific Northwest.

At a time when most women never traveled more than a few miles from home, Narcissa had already crossed a continent.

A Calling That Defied Convention

Her story began in western New York as the daughter of a prosperous farmer with a traditional, religious upbringing. Like many young women influenced by the religious fervor of the Second Great Awakening, she felt called to become a missionary. However, the American Board of Commissioners for Foreign Missions would not send unmarried women. If Narcissa wanted to serve God on the distant frontier, she would need a husband.

Marcus Whitman, a physician with missionary ambitions of his own, met Narcissa only briefly before their marriage. Their union was friendly, dutiful, and built more on shared purpose than romance. Just days after their 1836 wedding, they joined a missionary caravan and headed west: Narcissa was determined to be the first white woman to cross the Rocky Mountains.

The Long Road

Narcissa kept a journal in which she detailed her early, cautious optimism about a woman leaving everything behind. In a letter dated March 19, 1836, shortly before departing on the westward journey, she wrote: "I am contented and happy... I must expect trials, and be prepared for them."[1]

As the caravan traveled west, Narcissa insisted on riding sidesaddle. When the terrain grew rough, she walked for miles in her long skirts. Dust storms blinded her, water became scarce, and even the little food they had became spoiled. Still, she kept going, motivated by the belief that these hardships were part of God's plan.

To many emigrants she met along the trail, Narcissa became a symbol of possibility, proof that women could cross the plains, climb the Rockies, and carve out new lives far from eastern towns.

First Woman Over the Rockies

When Narcissa and another missionary's wife, Eliza Spalding, reached the summit of the Rockies, they became the first two white women known to have done so.[2] This moment, later mythologized in newspapers and missionary reports, inspired many more women to consider the overland trails as a path toward new beginnings.

First White Women Over The Rockies, Vol 1
Clifford Merrill Drury, Published by The Arthur H. Clark
Company, 1963

Narcissa Whitman reached the Columbia Plateau in early September 1836, marking the end of her five-month, 3,000-mile overland journey. The group's arrival at Fort Walla Walla on September 1, 1836, was not the triumphant homecoming Narcissa had envisioned. The Hudson's Bay Company outpost was a rugged collection of adobe-style buildings surrounded by palisades, mainly inhabited by fur traders, Native families, and laborers. She rested here only briefly before being escorted upriver to her mission site at Waiilatpu.

Daughter of the Grasslands

Waiilatpu ("place of the rye grass") was remote, windy, and far more primitive than Narcissa had anticipated. The mission consisted of a single log-and-adobe house, a small shed, and fields scratched into tough plateau soil. Narcissa described the homestead as "a lonely outpost on the great plain,"[3] surrounded by Nez Perce and Cayuse families whose rhythms of life were entirely different from her New York upbringing.

While her arrival on the Columbia Plateau marked the end of one hardship, it was the beginning of an even more demanding chapter of cultural negotiation, physical deprivation, and missionary labor on a landscape that would profoundly reshape her life.

Whitman Mission at Waiilatpu by William Henry Jackson, Courtesy National Park Service (SCBL 151) Used for Educational Purposes

Life Among the Cayuse

Narcissa's days were spent in grueling daily routines. She rose before dawn to start the fire (often made from twisted hay or buffalo chips when wood was scarce), prepared breakfast, milked the cow, tended the garden, hauled water from a well that might be a quarter-mile away, made butter, baked bread, mended clothes, educated children, and helped in the fields during planting and harvest. This wasn't occasional labor—this was every single day, in scorching summers and brutal winters, through illness and pregnancy, year after year.

While Narcissa taught school, managed the household, and struggled with isolation, she also tried to teach Christianity, domestic skills, and English to Cayuse women and children, but cultural misunderstandings ran deep. She viewed her mission as a spiritual rescue, but the Cayuse saw her as an outsider who misunderstood their world.

Tragedy at Waiilatpu

By the fall of 1847, Waiilatpu was overwhelmed by illness. Measles spread across the Columbia Plateau, carried west by wagon trains. While white emigrants often survived, likely due to stronger immune responses, the Cayuse and other Native communities experienced devastating deaths among their children, who died within days, sometimes hours.

Marcus Whitman, who had limited medical training, treated both emigrants and the Cayuse, but the outcomes were starkly unequal. As dozens of Cayuse children died under his care, suspicion and grief turned into anger. Many

Cayuse believed Whitman was poisoning their people, and longstanding tensions over land loss, mission control, livestock damage, and cultural clashes came to the surface.

On November 29, 1847, a small group of Cayuse men entered the mission under the pretense of seeking medicine and began to attack.[4]

Marcus Whitman was struck first, clubbed, and shot near the mission house. Narcissa witnessed the violence and attempted to flee, but she was shot outside the doorway. Still breathing, she was carried inside by two young men she had taught, then placed on a bed where she lingered for several hours before dying.

Eleven others at the station were killed over the next two days, including teachers, laborers, and recent emigrant families who had taken refuge at the mission. The violence was not indiscriminate; some were targeted because the Cayuse believed they had brought or spread the disease, while others were killed attempting to defend the station.

Nearly fifty women and children survived the attack and were taken captive. For more than a month, the survivors lived under Cayuse control—scared, hungry, and grieving—while negotiations went on between the Cayuse, Hudson's Bay Company officers, and leaders at Fort Vancouver.

The captives were finally ransomed by the Hudson's Bay Company in late December 1847, ending a traumatic ordeal but sparking what became known as the Cayuse War. The attack devastated the Protestant mission effort in the area, altered U.S.–Cayuse relations, and made Narcissa Whitman one of the most mythologized women of the American West.

The event became known as the Whitman Massacre, a story retold for decades as a martyrdom narrative in missionary publications and Western histories. But beneath the mythology lay a deeper truth: two cultures collided, and disease, desperation, and misunderstanding ignited tragedy.

Legacy of a Frontier Woman

Narcissa Whitman's life remains complex. She was brave, devout, and determined. She was also a product of her time: confident in her beliefs, certain of her calling, and unable to foresee how profoundly the arrival of settlers would alter Indigenous lives.

Yet her journey west opened the door for thousands of emigrants who followed. Her letters and journals remain some of the earliest and most vivid accounts written by a woman on the western frontier.

On the prairie, in the mountains, and in the contested lands of the Pacific Northwest, Narcissa Whitman lived a life of conviction. She crossed a continent, shaped a movement, and she paid the ultimate price for her presence at the crossroads of two worlds.

[1] Narcissa Whitman, letters to her parents, March 19 and December 5, 1836, in Letters of Narcissa Whitman, 1836–1847, ed. Clifford M. Drury (Portland: Oregon Historical Society, 1986), 7, 32.
[2] Clifford M. Drury, Where Wagons Could Go: Narcissa Whitman and Eliza Spalding (Lincoln: University of Nebraska Press, 1969), 112–113, 267–275.
[3] Narcissa Whitman, letter to her parents, December 5, 1836, in Letters of Narcissa Whitman, 1836–1847, ed. Clifford M. Drury (Portland: Oregon Historical Society, 1986), 32.
[4] M. R. H. Brown and Robert H. Ruby, The Cayuse Indians: Imperial Tribesmen of Old Oregon (Norman: University of Oklahoma Press, 1972), 157–170.

Chapter 4 — Laura Ingalls Wilder: The Real Woman Behind the Myth

"To forsake culture, plenty, prosperity and peace, for crude living, poverty, adversity and war, requires a poise of soul few possess."

— Joanna L. Stratton

LAURA INGALLS WILDER IS one of the most recognizable names in American frontier history, yet the story most people know is not the one she actually lived.

Her *Little House* books created an enduring image of plucky pioneers, wholesome hardships, and the warm glow of family perseverance. But the reality of Laura's life on the prairie was far more difficult, uncertain, and shaped by near-constant instability.

Before she became an author in her sixties, Laura endured a lifetime of failed crops, harsh winters, fires, drought, disease, hunger, and the relentless insecurity that defined frontier poverty. Her story is a testament to resilience.

Growing Up on the Move

Laura was born in 1867 in Pepin County, Wisconsin, into a family that seemed always on the brink of moving west again. Charles "Pa" Ingalls was restless, drawn toward new opportunities and open spaces. The family lived in Wisconsin, Kansas, Minnesota, Iowa, and Dakota Territory, sometimes staying only a single season before uprooting again.

Laura later softened these moves in her books, but the truth was harder: In Walnut Grove, Minnesota, the family initially lived in a dugout sod house on a preemption claim. After spending the winter there, they moved into a newly built house on the same land. Two consecutive summers of crop failure forced them to relocate to Iowa. The family ultimately left Minnesota after a devastating grasshopper plague. In Kansas, they built a house illegally on Osage land and left when federal authorities ordered squatters off the reservation.

Dugout home. Public Domain.

In Iowa, the family endured dire poverty, sickness, and debt so crushing that they fled town without paying the rent.

Their real frontier life was not a series of wholesome adventures; it was survival under constant pressure.

Disease, Loss, and the Reality of Frontier Childhood

Laura's books mention illness, but the real danger was far worse. The Ingalls children battled malaria, scarlet fever, and recurring fevers from contaminated water. Her sister Mary suffered a stroke-like fever that left her permanently blind—an event Laura described tenderly in her books, but which was a devastating blow to the family's future.

Poverty meant there was no safety net. When crops failed, they starved. When sickness swept the prairie, they endured it without doctors. When a child fell ill, the family often had to keep working regardless.

Through it all, Laura learned self-reliance.

By age ten, she could ride bareback, set traps, sew clothing, and prepare meals. She chopped wood, carried water, and worked long hours to support the family. Her girlhood was not idyllic; it was defined by labor.

The Long Winter: Truth Behind the Pages

The winter of 1880–81, remembered locally as The Hard Winter, was one of the most severe ever recorded in the Dakota Territory. Beginning in October 1880, blizzard after blizzard swept across the prairie with barely a pause in between. Snow piled so high that rail lines disappeared beneath drifts, making it impossible for trains to reach the isolated settlement of De Smet, where the Ingalls family lived.

By December, every rail route into town was shut down. Supply trains stranded hundreds of miles away left the community completely cut off. Food, coal, kerosene, flour, and clothing dwindled quickly. Merchants rationed what little was left, and families made do by burning twisted hay sticks when coal ran out and grinding wheat in hand mills or coffee grinders to produce coarse flour.

The Ingalls family lived in a small, drafty building that shook in the wind. When the storms came, and they came often, whiteout conditions sometimes lasted two or three days at a time, making it impossible to see even a few feet past the doorway. Laura later wrote that the house became so cold that water froze indoors, and their breath hung in the air.

By February, the situation turned desperate. They rationed wheat to teaspoons per person, stretching meals hour by hour. "We measured it out as though it were gold dust," she later wrote. There were days when the family survived on nothing but coarse bread and small potatoes.[1]

In one of the most well-documented acts of heroism from that winter, Cap Garland and Almanzo Wilder risked their lives to ride out into the frozen prairie in search of a hidden homesteader who was rumored to have stored wheat. Their successful return prevented mass starvation in the town.

When the final blizzard hit in March 1881, families had already endured nearly five months of continuous storms. Only in April, when the railroad was finally dug out and trains arrived, did the crisis end.

For Laura, who was fifteen that winter, the Hard Winter became one of the defining experiences of her frontier youth and an ordeal that shaped her views on endurance, community, and survival.

She later softened the violence of hunger and the terror of isolation for younger readers, but the truth was stark: that winter altered her understanding of the prairie forever.

Desmet, Dakota Territory Map, 1883 Used for Public Educational Purposes

Young Teacher

On December 10, 1882, just weeks before her sixteenth birthday, Laura Ingalls accepted her first teaching position at the Bouchie School (sometimes spelled Brewster School) in Kingsbury County, Dakota Territory. She was 15 years old, legally allowed to teach only because she had passed the county examination. Wilder later recalled that she took the position out of necessity rather than ambition: the family needed money, and opportunities for young women to earn wages on the frontier were extremely limited.[2]

Her early teaching experiences were difficult. The Brewster School was a remote, one-room school, and the winter was severe. Wilder lived away from home with a quarrelsome boarding family, an experience she described as "dreadful"

47

in later writings.[3] She taught for short terms, returned home when school sessions ended, and took whatever work she could find to contribute to the household.

Between 1883 and 1885, she alternated among teaching rural schools, working for the town dressmaker in De Smet, and attending De Smet High School when family finances allowed. Her schooling was intermittent, and though she completed substantial coursework, she did not graduate.

These were formative years. They reveal the economic pressures frontier girls faced and the narrow range of respectable paid work available to them.

Marriage, Loss, and a New Kind of Hardship

At eighteen, Laura married Almanzo Wilder. Their early years together were harder than any she had lived through as a girl.

Their infant son died after only a few weeks. Almanzo was partially paralyzed by diphtheria. Their crops burned, their house burned, and their farm failed. They lived temporarily in a one-room rented house in De Smet, barely surviving.

It was not until they moved to Mansfield, Missouri, that they found stability, but even there, prosperity came slowly, built on decades of work, frugality, and improvisation.

The Making of a Writer

Laura did not begin writing professionally until she was in her sixties. The Great Depression had wiped out the family's savings, and writing offered a way to help support herself and Almanzo.

Her daughter, Rose Wilder Lane, encouraged her to turn childhood memories into books. The result was a series that reshaped the American imagination.

But the writing process was not simply nostalgia. Laura intentionally refined her childhood into a narrative of hope, perseverance, and moral character, the values she believed America desperately needed during the Depression and war years.

But she left out the darkest moments. She softened her father's failures, omitted stories of violence, poverty, and emotional strain. In doing so, she created not a precise memoir, but an idealized frontier mythology.

The Real Laura's Legacy

Laura Ingalls Wilder's life taught her that survival on the prairie demanded more than optimism. It required strength, labor, and an ability to endure disappointment without surrendering hope.

Her diaries, letters, and the experiences of her adult life reveal a woman who knew true fear, lived true hunger, built and rebuilt her life many times, and held onto a belief in family, community, and perseverance.

In the Little House books, readers experience warmth and adventure. In Laura's real life, historians face a deeper, tougher, and more complex frontier, one shaped not by charming stories but by genuine resilience.

She remains one of the most influential frontier women not because of how she lived as a child, but because of how she told her story as an adult—with honesty shaped by memory, restraint shaped by loss, and courage shaped by years of survival.

Laura Ingalls Wilder, circa 1885, Public Domain

[1] Laura Ingalls Wilder, Pioneer Girl: The Annotated Autobiography, ed. Pamela Smith Hill (Sioux Falls: South Dakota Historical Society Press, 2014), 153–175.

[2] Pamela Smith Hill, Laura Ingalls Wilder: A Writer's Life (New York: HarperCollins, 2007), 46–56.

[3] William Anderson, Laura Ingalls Wilder: A Biography (New York: HarperCollins, 1994), 44–52.

Chapter 5 —Susan Shelby Magoffin: The Wandering Princess

"I go to the West, where men and women are made strong by the land."

— Margaret Fuller

ON JUNE 11, 1846, Susan Shelby Magoffin left Independence, Missouri, riding in a carriage luxuriously appointed with every comfort her husband could provide. She was eighteen, pregnant, and married to a wealthy trader named Samuel Magoffin. Unlike Amelia Knight, who walked beside an ox team in the mud, Susan traveled in a private carriage with a maid, a coop of live chickens, and a daily supply of fresh milk from her own cows.

On the first pages of her diary, she called herself a "wandering princess." It was a title she used without irony. She grew up on a Kentucky plantation, the granddaughter of Isaac Shelby, the state's first governor. She had never cooked a meal, made a bed, or known a single day of physical hardship.[1]

Now she was heading into the heart of the American Southwest at the precise moment the United States declared war on Mexico.

Her diary, kept from June 1846 to September 1847, is not a survival chronicle like Amelia Knight's. It is a coming-of-age story. It records the collision of a sheltered Southern belle with the brutal realities of the frontier, a clash that would strip away her vanity, her health, and ultimately, her child.

The Princess on the Prairie

The early weeks of the journey were a grand adventure. The Magoffin caravan was immense: fourteen wagons, each pulled by six yoke of oxen, a baggage wagon, a carriage for Susan, and twenty men to drive the stock and guard the train. At night, her servants pitched a large tent, laid down a carpet, and set up a proper bed with a mattress. They cooked her meals and served them on a table.[2]

"It is the life of a wandering princess, mine," she wrote on June 15. "When I do not wish to get out myself to pick flowers, the Mexican servants riding on mules pick them for me."

She treated the prairie as a park made for her amusement. She marveled at the buffalo ("ugly, ill-shapen things"), collected pebbles, and wrote about the "romance" of the trail. But the frontier did not care about her status.

A Turn for the Worse

On July 4, reality set in when her carriage crashed.

They were crossing a creek bank when the vehicle tipped over, throwing Susan and her belongings into the dirt. "I was very much frightened," she wrote, but she was unhurt. It was the first crack in the facade of her protected journey.

Then the weather turned vicious. The heat was suffocating, and the mosquitoes were relentless. On July 21, a violent storm struck their camp. The wind tore the stakes of their tent from the ground. The heavy canvas collapsed over Susan and Samuel as they lay in bed. Rain poured in, soaking the carpet and the bedding. The "princess" was left shivering in the mud, waiting for her servants to rescue her.

Bent's Fort and the Loss

By late July, after nearly six weeks of travel, the caravan reached Bent's Fort, a massive adobe trading post on the Arkansas River in present-day Colorado. It was a chaotic, noisy place, filled with traders, trappers, Cheyenne and Arapaho families, and soldiers from the Army of the West preparing to invade New Mexico. "The outside fills my idea of an ancient castle…[and] we have two windows, one looking out on the plain," she wrote of her accommodations. But Susan was feeling ill.

The bouncing of the carriage and the strain of the journey had taken a toll on her pregnancy. On July 30, she turned nineteen. She celebrated in her room at the fort, perhaps the only white woman in a thousand miles of wilderness.

The next day, July 31, the diary entry is stark.

"The mysteries of a new world have been shown to me," she wrote. "In a few short months I should have been a happy mother and made the heart of a father glad, but the ruling hand of a mighty Providence has interposed and by an abortion deprived us of the hope, the fond hope of mortals."

Susan's recreated room in the upstairs corner of the fort (NPS photo

She had suffered a miscarriage.[3]

The emotional shock and physical pain were immense. For the first time, Susan Magoffin was no longer a spectator; she was a participant in the harsh reality of the West. There were no doctors to help her, only the rough comfort of the fort. She stayed in her room for days, listening to the noise of the plaza below with its gambling, swearing, and the constant movement of men and animals.

In a moment that highlights the strange collisions of the frontier, she noted in her diary that while she lay recovering, a Native American woman in a room below her gave birth to a healthy baby. Within thirty minutes, the new mother took the infant down to the river to bathe. Susan marveled at the woman's strength, contrasting it with her own fragility.

Into Santa Fe

But they had come too far to turn back. Samuel Magoffin's business was in Santa Fe and Chihuahua, and the war meant high profits for traders who could get their goods through. So, on August 8, while Susan was still weak, they left Bent's Fort and headed south into the mountains.

The "wandering princess" was gone. The woman who rode into New Mexico in the summer of 1846 was more disciplined, perceptive, and distinctly less provincial. Her own diary shows the shift.

On August 31, 1846, they entered Santa Fe, just days after the city's capture, and rented a house near the plaza. Susan became a figure of fascination to the local women, who had never seen an American woman in her hoop skirts and corsets. They touched her clothes, examined her hair, and asked endless questions.

Susan, in turn, watched them. She was scandalized by the women who smoked cigarettes and gambled at the Monte tables, particularly Doña Tules, the legendary saloon owner and power broker of Santa Fe. "A stately dame of a certain age," Susan called her, noting with disapproval that she possessed "that shrewd sense and fascinating manner necessary to allure the wayward, inexperienced youth to the final ruin."

In August, she wrote that she was beginning to "catch the language" and could manage simple exchanges in Spanish, something she said gave her "much advantage in market matters." Her wardrobe changed as quickly as her worldview. She noted with amusement that she had exchanged her Kentucky bonnet for a rebozo, the long cotton shawl worn by Mexican women, because it was practical in the heat and dust and helped her move "unnoticed among the Señoras."

View of Santa Fe Plaza in the 1850's, ca. 1930 — Gerald Cassidy (1869–1934) Used for Educational Purposes

Food became another point of education. On first trying guiso verde, the green chile stew she saw served everywhere, she admitted it was "much too strong for my stomach," but within weeks she was eating chile-based dishes daily, sometimes "as greedily as the Mexicans," noting that the spice helped her endure the altitude and long days.

Her observations extended beyond domestic details. After the U.S. occupation of New Mexico by General Stephen Watts Kearny, she recorded the merging of military and civilian life in Santa Fe, such as soldiers drilling in the plaza, merchants reopening stalls under U.S. protection, and local families cautiously approaching the American camp. Her diary entries from late August reflect Kearny's own field reports, describing a population "quiet and well-disposed," though cautious of the sudden change in authority.[4]

By the end of her stay in New Mexico, the young bride who had once seen Mexico as foreign and faintly threatening now recorded sympathy for the people's poverty, admiration for their resilience, and a growing awareness of the cultural complexity around her. The transformation is traceable line by line in her diary.

She had undergone an incredible transformation. From the life of a privileged teenager, she now knew how to make tortillas, knit, and spent her days visiting with the women of Santa Fe, navigating the complex social hierarchy of an occupied city.

The Shadow of War

The war followed them like a shadow. The Magoffins moved south in the wake of Colonel Alexander Doniphan's First Missouri Mounted Volunteers, whose 1846–47 campaign carved a path from New Mexico into Chihuahua.

Susan recorded the constant presence of soldiers on the trail, the columns of volunteers, forage parties, Mexican scouts, and detachments carrying dispatches. Wagons rumbled past carrying wounded men from earlier clashes. She noted seeing "the very places the battle had been fought" near the vicinity of Brazito, where Doniphan had defeated Mexican forces on December 25, 1846.

As the caravan moved toward El Paso del Norte and then deeper into Chihuahua, the war became more visible and more brutal. Doniphan's men shared accounts of the fight at the Battle of the Sacramento on February 28, 1847, one of the most decisive victories of the entire New Mexico campaign, describing abandoned gun pits, shattered artillery, and Mexican dead left along the rocky ridge. Merchants and civilians traveling with the army, including the Magoffins, witnessed the aftermath of foraging raids, burned ranchos, and the strain on local families suddenly caught between two armies.

The physical toll on Susan intensified.

Through late 1846 and 1847 she endured repeated bouts of what she called "fever," a term period physicians used loosely but which fits malaria, typhoid, or dysentery, all too common along the Rio Grande during the war. She wrote of days when she could not sit upright, when chills racked her body, and when medicine chests were nearly empty. During this period, she was pregnant again, adding danger to every mile of travel.[5]

By summer 1847, the Magoffins had reached Matamoros, a major U.S. Army depot on the lower Rio Grande. The city was in the grip of a widespread yellow fever epidemic documented in both military hospital records and local parish registers. Susan fell ill in early September. Her symptoms of severe fever, black vomit, and delirium match classic 19th-century descriptions of vomito negro, the feared tropical form of yellow fever.[6]

60

Her handwriting weakens across the pages, then it stops. Her final diary entry is dated September 8, 1847.

The rest of the story comes from other sources. After she had contracted yellow fever, she gave birth to a son, who died shortly thereafter. Susan's health was forever compromised from the ordeal.

The End of the Trail

Susan and Samuel Magoffin eventually returned to the United States, settling near St. Louis, hoping the change of climate would help her recover. It did not.

Susan Shelby Magoffin died on October 26, 1855. She was twenty-eight years old.

She left behind her diary, a leather-bound book filled with the observations of a girl who became a woman on the Santa Fe Trail. It remains one of the most important accounts of the West, not because it chronicles battles or treaties, but because it captures the intimate, human cost of expansion.

She had gone west looking for romance. She found dust, pain, and loss. And in recording it all—the crashed carriage, the collapsed tent, the lost child, the gambling women of Santa Fe—she left a testimony far more enduring than the "wandering princess" she had set out to be.

Susan's voice is distinct from the other women of her time. She had privilege, yes. She had servants and a carriage. But the prairie stripped those defenses away one by one. By the end, she was just another woman on the frontier, fighting to keep her child, fighting to keep her health, and ultimately, fighting to be heard.

Susan Shelby Magoffin

[1] Susan Shelby Magoffin, Down the Santa Fe Trail and Into Mexico: The Diary of Susan Shelby Magoffin, 1846–1847 (New Haven: Yale University Press, 1962).
[2] William W. Dunmire and Regina C. Dunmire, New Mexico's Spanish and Mexican Colonial Foodways (Santa Fe: Museum of New Mexico Press, 1994), 112–113.
[3] Susan Shelby Magoffin, diary, winter 1846–47.
[4] William W. Dunmire and Regina C. Dunmire, New Mexico's Spanish and Mexican Colonial Foodways (Santa Fe: Museum of New Mexico Press, 1994), 112–113.
[5] Magoffin, Diary, winter 1846–47
[6] "Yellow Fever Cases in Matamoros, 1847," in Medical and Surgical History of the War with Mexico (Washington, DC: Surgeon General's Office, 1849), 22–27.

Part II — Women Between Worlds:
Captivity, Adoption, and the Human Cost of
Cultural Collision

Chapter 6 — Cynthia Ann Parker: Captured by Comanche, Mother of a Future Chief, Torn Between Worlds

"Remember us—for we lived, and worked, and hoped on this land."

—Ella Cara Deloria

CYNTHIA ANN PARKER'S LIFE sits at the fault line between two nations and two ways of living, a single woman's story that carries the weight of a whole era of conflict on the southern Plains. Captured as a child by Comanches, adopted and married among them, and then retaken—this time by Texas Rangers—she became a symbol for both sides, even as she herself never stopped longing for the world that was taken from her.

Early Life

Cynthia Ann was born around 1826 in Illinois to Silas and Lucy Parker, a frontier Baptist family that moved to central Texas in 1833. They helped build Fort Parker, a rough stockade on the Navasota River in present-day Limestone County, intended as a shelter from growing raids on settler cabins.

Fort Parker, 1836

The attack on Parker's Fort, later known simply as Fort Parker, was not a random raid. Throughout the spring of 1836, Comanche and Kiowa bands were moving across the central Texas frontier in response to escalating Anglo settlement and the breakdown of earlier trading arrangements. The Parkers' settlement, built in 1834 near the headwaters of the Navasota River, sat on land long used by Comanche groups for hunting and travel. Despite warnings from neighboring settlers and increasing reports of raiding along the Brazos, the fort remained lightly defended. Most of the adult men were working in fields some distance away that morning, leaving only a small guard inside the stockade.

On May 19, 1836, a large mounted group of Comanche, Kiowa, and Kichai warriors—with contemporary witnesses estimating their numbers from about 100 to several hundred—approached the gate. A white flag or cloth was raised, consistent with earlier Comanche signals used to initiate negotiations. Believing that a talk might prevent bloodshed, the Parkers sent Benjamin Parker, one of the family's leaders, to meet them outside the walls. He walked out unarmed, hoping to buy time for women and children to escape into the woods. The warriors quickly surrounded him and killed him.

The mounted fighters then charged the fort's open gate. James W. Parker and Silas M. Parker attempted to rally a defense but were quickly overwhelmed. Silas was killed near the entrance; his brother Samuel died while trying to cover his family's retreat. During the brief, chaotic assault, at least five men were killed and several others wounded. Most of the women and older children escaped on foot into the surrounding woods, as Benjamin Parker had planned.

In the rush through the gate, however, the attackers seized five captives. Cynthia Ann Parker was taken from the yard near the main cabin. Her younger brother, John, was captured while trying to follow his fleeing relatives, and Rachel Plummer was seized after attempting to defend her infant; both she and her baby were taken. A neighbor woman, Elizabeth Kellogg, who had sought refuge at the fort during rising frontier tensions, was also carried away. Other attempts at abduction were made, but many were able to slip into the woods before the warriors could encircle them.[1]

Fort Parker, 1836

The raid ended as quickly as it began. Within minutes, the mounted force departed with their prisoners and loot, riding north toward the upper Red River country.

A rescue party from nearby settlements arrived too late to pursue. Early reports quickly spread through Texas newspapers and military records, marking the event as one of the most devastating attacks on an Anglo frontier family up to that point. The fate of the captives became part of

Texas legend. Rachel Plummer's ordeal was chronicled in her 1838 narrative, and Elizabeth Kellogg was eventually ransomed. However, Cynthia Ann was taken deep into the Comanchería.

Becoming Naduah

The raiders took Cynthia and the other captives north into Comanche country, across the rolling plains that Anglo maps left mostly blank. For Cynthia Ann, the first months were likely brutal; many accounts note that new captives, especially children, were tested harshly before being accepted or traded.

Why They Took Captives

Comanche bands raided extensively across Texas, New Mexico, and northern Mexico, and captives were a standard part of these raids. The primary goals of the raids were horses, loot, and power, but they also resulted in the taking of people, especially children and young women.

High death rates from disease and warfare, along with low fertility among Comanche women, meant that bringing outsiders into the group helped maintain their numbers. Captives were used as labor (herding, camp work, trading) and, if young enough, might eventually be fully adopted into the tribe.

In other words, captives were not just "spoils"; they were a way to rebuild families, labor force, and warriors.

The Harsh Beginning

The first weeks or months after capture could be exceedingly rough, and many never lived long enough to be adopted. Children who cried or could not keep up might be abandoned or killed, especially infants, because they put the raiding party at risk.

Those who survived this initial period, like Cynthia Ann, faced harsh tests: beatings, heavy work, close surveillance, and a complete loss of language and familiar customs.

Adoption into the Band

If a captive, especially a child like Cynthia Ann, survived long enough, the situation could eventually change for the better. In her case, she was adopted into a Nokoni Comanche family and given a new name, Naduah, which is often translated as "someone found" or "she who carries herself with grace."

Over the next twenty years, she stopped being an outsider and became fully Comanche in language, dress, and loyalty. She married the war chief Peta Nocona, the son of the notable chief Iron Jacket, likely when she was in her early teens. Unlike many successful chiefs, he is remembered for having taken no other wives. They had three children together: sons Quanah and Pecos (often called Pecan), and a daughter, Topsannah, "Prairie Flower."

From the view inside Comanche society, Cynthia Ann was no longer a captive but a respected wife and mother in a powerful band that ranged the Staked Plains and raided deep into Texas and Mexico. From the view of Texas settlers, she remained the lost child of Fort Parker, a living reminder of the dangers at the edge of settlement, and her uncle James Parker spent years in vain expeditions trying to recover her.

Cynthia Ann Parker, "Naduah"

Pease River Massacre, 1860

By 1860, the line of Anglo settlement had moved deep into former Comanche hunting country.

Decades of raids, counter-raids, and retaliatory expeditions had produced a cycle of escalating violence in which neither side trusted the other, and every frontier alarm triggered calls for punitive action. That autumn, reports of stolen livestock near the Pease River drew the attention of state forces. Lawrence Sullivan "Sul" Ross, then a young Ranger officer serving under the authority of the frontier defense system, was operating in coordination with elements of the U.S. 2nd Cavalry along the Clear Fork of the Brazos.

On December 18, 1860, scouts located a small Comanche encampment near Mule Creek, a tributary of the Pease River. Contemporary accounts, including Ross's official report, claimed the villagers numbered between 12 and 25 warriors and portrayed the engagement as a decisive blow against a hostile band preparing new raids.

However, later examinations of the campsite, analysis of Comanche oral histories, and comparison with military casualty reports point to a different picture. The camp consisted of approximately nine lodges, indicative of a small family group, engaged in butchering buffalo. Most adult men were absent on a hunting foray.

The attacking force, composed of Ross's Rangers and a detachment of U.S. Army troops under Captain Nicholas Nolan, struck at dawn, catching the camp entirely by surprise. The fight lasted only minutes. Soldiers and Rangers killed several people, most of them women and children, in the first rush. Many fled northward across the flats toward the river breaks as mounted Rangers pursued. Later Ranger retellings, published in the 1870s–1890s, embellished the action into a significant battle, describing dozens of warriors killed; these claims do not align with archaeological evidence or the camp's small size described in the original field reports.

Modern historians largely agree that the encounter was not a confrontation with a large war party, but rather the destruction of a small, vulnerable Comanche family group temporarily encamped while processing meat.

Amid the chaos, a fleeing Comanche woman carrying a small girl was chased down. When Rangers subdued her, they noticed she had blue eyes and light hair. Under questioning and with the help of interpreters, she was eventually identified as Cynthia Ann Parker. Her young daughter, Prairie Flower, was taken with her. Her sons, including Quanah, were not in the camp and had escaped with other warriors elsewhere on the Plains.

Texas newspapers and officials celebrated the "rescue" as a victory, claiming a white woman was recovered after twenty-four years "among the savages." For Cynthia Ann herself, every remaining account indicates it was just another captivity.

A Life Between Worlds

After Pease River, authorities moved her through a series of households and towns, sometimes putting her and Prairie Flower on display in public spaces where curious onlookers paid to see the "white Indian woman." Eventually, she was placed with relatives in East Texas, including the O'Quinn family, where well-meaning kin tried to "civilize" her by cutting her hair, dressing her in calico, and insisting she live as a farm wife and Christian.

Tintype, Cynthia Ann Parker, "Naduah" 1861

But Cynthia Ann never truly reintegrated into Anglo society. Visitors and family members recalled that she mourned for her Comanche husband, whom Texas lore claimed had died at Pease River but whom several modern historians believe survived and later died of other causes. She grieved for her missing sons, especially Quanah, whose name she would repeat as she looked toward the west.

She reportedly refused to speak English, responded in Comanche, and repeatedly tried to escape back to her people, only to be returned to Texas again and again.

Her last connection to her Comanche life was her daughter, Prairie Flower "Topsannah," who grew up as a fragile child and, in 1864, succumbed to influenza and pneumonia. Not long before or after, depending on the account, news reached Cynthia Ann that her son Pecos had died of smallpox among the Comanche.

Those losses broke what remained of her will. Relatives reported that after Prairie Flower's death, Cynthia Ann began to refuse food, eating less and less, as if turning away from a world she had never chosen. She died sometime between 1864 and 1871; most scholarly summaries place her death around March 1871, likely from influenza complicated by malnutrition, at a family home in East Texas. She was buried in a small country cemetery near present-day Poynor or Henderson County.[2]

The Son Who Remembered

While Cynthia Ann's final years played out in obscurity, her oldest son, Quanah, rose to become one of the last great war leaders of the Comanche.

As railroads and buffalo hunters poured onto the Plains in the 1870s, he led resistance from the Llano Estacado, guiding his band through a shrinking world until starvation and relentless military campaigns forced surrender.

After arriving at the reservation in 1875, Quanah Parker became a bridging figure, advocating for his people, visiting Washington, D.C., and even working with white ranchers, all while never forgetting his mother. In 1910, decades after her death, he arranged to have Cynthia Ann's remains and Prairie Flower's reinterred at the Post Oak Mission Cemetery near Cache, Oklahoma, and later their graves were moved once more to Fort Sill.

On her new headstone, she was named not just as a Parker but as the mother of Quanah, the Comanche chief who carried both her worlds into his own life.

Torn Between Stories

For over a century, others have used Cynthia Ann Parker to tell different versions of the frontier: novels and films like The Searchers have portrayed her as a symbol of lost innocence or heroic rescue. Historians now work to peel away those layers and uncover what little is actually known about the woman herself.

Cynthia Ann's return to the Parkers was not a restoration but an interruption. She had already built a full life, including her own family and kinship within the Noconi. The tragedy was not that she belonged nowhere, but that she was taken from the place where she did belong. Her fate illustrates how the expansion of the Texas frontier not only destroyed Comanche autonomy but also tore apart families on both sides, forcing individuals like Cynthia Ann into lives they neither chose nor recognized as their own.

Ultimately, her story resists any tidy narrative. What happened to her stemmed from two traumatic ruptures: one that tore her from her family of birth and another that severed her from the family she had built. The cost was borne by her and by everyone connected to her—from her Comanche husband and children to the Parkers, who never fully grasped her trauma. Her life stands as a testament to what the frontier took from individuals on every side.

---

[1] Rachel Plummer, Narrative of the Capture and Subsequent Sufferings of Mrs. Rachel Plummer (Houston: Telegraph Power Press, 1838).
[2] James W. Parker, The True Account of the Capture and Rescue of Cynthia Ann Parker (various pamphlet editions, 1840s–1860s).

Chapter 7— Susan La Flesche Picotte, First Native American Woman Physician in the United States

"It is the women who will lead the healing among the tribes. Inside them are the powers of love and strength given by the Moon and the Earth. When everyone else gives up, it is the women who sings the songs of strength. She is the backbone of the people. So, to our women we say, sing your songs of strength; pray for your special powers; keep our people strong; be respectful, gentle, and modest."

—Village Wise Man, Lakota

SUSAN LA FLESCHE PICOTTE practiced medicine on a different kind of frontier—not one of wagon ruts and cavalry charges, but of crowded agency offices, schoolrooms, and one-room log houses where Omaha families fought off disease and dispossession at the same time. As the first Native American woman in the United States to earn a medical degree, she used her training to heal bodies and, just as urgently, to argue in letters, reports, and meetings that her people were citizens with land, rights, and a future.

Growing Up Between Worlds

Susan was born on June 17, 1865, on the Omaha Reservation in northeast Nebraska, during the first generation of life under the reservation system. She was the youngest daughter of Joseph La Flesche (Inshta Theumba, or Iron Eye), the Omaha tribal leader who pushed his people toward farming, formal education, and citizenship as a means of survival.

Iron Eye was of Ponca ancestry with some French Canadian heritage. Educated in St. Louis, Missouri, he returned to the reservation as a young man and identified culturally as Omaha. In 1853, Chief Big Elk adopted him and designated him as his successor. By about 1855, Iron Eye had become the principal leader of the Omaha. He supported limited assimilation—most notably land allotment—which generated internal tension within the tribe.[1]

Susan's mother, Mary Gale, was the daughter of Dr. John Gale, a white U.S. Army surgeon stationed at Fort Atkinson, and Nicomi, a woman of Omaha, Otoe, and Iowa heritage. Although Mary understood both French and English, she reportedly only spoke Omaha.[2]

The family lived in a frame house, wore Euro-American clothing, and sent their children to mission schools, yet still spoke Omaha and followed many tribal customs.

As a girl, Susan watched the collision of cultures in intimate ways. One story she later recounted stayed with her for life: as a child, she sat by the bedside of a sick Omaha woman and saw the tribal messenger ride out to fetch the government doctor. He never came. The patient died before morning. She later said that the event convinced her she had to leave, study medicine, and return to care for her own people.

House of Susan La Flesche Picotte: Walt Hill, Omaha Reservation, Nebraska. 1878. She resided here from 1908 until 1915, when she died. Negative 54752 A, National Anthropological Archives, Smithsonian Institution.

It was an early lesson in how public policy, an underfunded Indian service, and a negligent physician translated directly into life and death on the reservation.

Her father encouraged his daughters to seek education as aggressively as his sons. Susan first attended the Presbyterian mission school on the reservation, then the Elizabeth Institute for Young Ladies in New Jersey, and later the Hampton Institute in Virginia, where she excelled in the Native American program and came into contact with reformers from the Women's National Indian Association. Those allies, impressed by her ability and seriousness, helped secure a scholarship for medical training.

Earning the M.D.

While women commonly served as healers in Omaha
society, it was rare for women in the United States to attend
medical school. In the late nineteenth century, only a small
number of institutions admitted women. Susan applied to
and was accepted by the Women's Medical College of
Pennsylvania in Philadelphia, founded in 1850 as one of the
few East Coast medical schools dedicated to educating
women.

In 1886, Susan began her studies in Philadelphia. The
journey itself, leaving the reservation, traveling east to a
crowded industrial city, was a cultural shock, but she
thrived academically, ranking at the top of her class. Her
coursework included anatomy, surgery, obstetrics, and
public health; in her spare time, she wrote letters home that
mixed homesickness with determination to finish the
degree.

When she graduated in 1889 with highest honors,
newspapers in both Native and white communities noted
the milestone: she was, by every available record, the first
Native American woman in the United States to earn an
M.D. After a brief internship at the Women's Hospital of
Philadelphia, she faced a choice familiar to many
first-generation professionals: stay in the city where pay
and status might be higher, or return to a home community
that needed her most. She chose to go back to Nebraska.

Reservation Doctor and Federal Employee

That fall, the Office of Indian Affairs appointed her as
"physician to the Omaha Agency," a government position

that offered a modest salary but carried huge responsibilities. From 1889 to 1893, she was the sole doctor for about 1,200 Omaha people spread over roughly 1,350 square miles of rolling prairie and bottomland. Her office was a small 12-by-16-foot room near the schoolyard, and her rounds were made on horseback or in a buggy, often during harsh winters and hot summers, with house calls extending late into the night.

Her daily work included treating infectious diseases—tuberculosis, trachoma, measles—setting fractures, delivering babies, and coping with injuries from farm accidents, all with limited supplies and no nearby hospital. At the same time, she handled the paperwork of a federal physician: monthly and annual reports on morbidity, vaccination, and sanitation; correspondence with the Office of Indian Affairs about shortages and needs; and interactions with mission boards and white reform societies that helped pay for vaccines and equipment.

From early on, Susan used those letters to press federal authorities for broader reforms. She described how overcrowded, poorly ventilated houses helped spread tuberculosis; how lack of clean water and proper waste disposal made intestinal diseases epidemic; and how alcoholism—fueled by local white bootleggers—was devastating Omaha families. In one 1907 letter to Commissioner of Indian Affairs Francis Leupp, she opened with the phrase that later gave a federal exhibit its title: "If you knew the conditions…" and then laid out, point by point, what had to change.

Between 1891 and 1893, she also held the title of "medical missionary" for the Women's National Indian Association, effectively juggling two overlapping roles: a government doctor and a church-supported health educator, within a single body and set of nerves. The strain was significant; she resigned her official agency position in 1893 due to exhaustion and chronic ear issues, but continued her private practice among the Omaha.

In 1894, Susan married Henry Picotte, a Yankton Sioux man who worked in local business and land dealings. They settled near Bancroft, Nebraska, and had two sons, Caryl and Pierre. She continued to practice medicine while raising her children, often bringing them along in the buggy on house calls. Her son later recalled that he and his brother "grew up in the back of a wagon" as she drove from patient to patient.

Land, Law, and Allotment

Susan's work as a physician constantly intersected with the politics of land. Under the Dawes Act and earlier Omaha-specific agreements, tribal lands were being divided into individual allotments, with "surplus" acreage opened to white purchase—a process that, in practice, often stripped Native people of some of their best ground. As an educated, bilingual woman, she became a key interpreter and advocate in this maze.

She helped families read and understand complex deeds and leases, explained how property taxes affected new citizen-landholders. Alcohol damage was another constant. Liquor dealers and land speculators used alcohol to manipulate Omaha landholders into signing away allotments or accepting unfavorable leases. Her husband, Henry, struggled with alcoholism himself and died in 1905; tuberculosis was also a factor in his death.

Susan La Flesche Picotte

These experiences sharpened her temperance activism. She supported prohibition measures in Thurston County, campaigned for federal laws restricting alcohol sales to

Native people with trust lands, and spoke publicly about the social and health costs of drinking.

In letters to the Office of Indian Affairs, she complained about "underhanded dealings" and called for stronger protections for widows and orphans whose allotments were at risk. She also championed state-level laws, like Nebraska's 1911 Gallagher Bill, to protect Native women's and children's inheritances—speaking in Omaha at tense community meetings until she gained support.

For Susan, public health and land rights were interconnected issues. When land was lost, families moved into poorer housing or left the community entirely, worsening illness and social decay. When people were pushed into wage labor far from home, they faced more exploitative conditions and an increased risk of disease. Her letters and speeches reveal a consistent link between medical diagnosis and political analysis.

Building a Hospital of Their Own

From her earliest days as a doctor, Susan dreamed of building a proper hospital on the reservation so severe cases wouldn't have to be sent to Omaha or Sioux City, or left untreated in remote log cabins. Federal Indian health services, already strained, offered no funds for such a project. So she turned to private philanthropy, church networks, and urban women's clubs, writing hundreds of letters and traveling to eastern cities to speak about the Omaha and their health needs.

By 1907, she had moved to Walthill, a small town on the edge of the reservation, where she selected it as the site for the future hospital. The Picotte family helped build their own house there, and Susan began using it as an informal clinic: people came for dressings, childbirth advice, and political meetings.

Years of fundraising paid off. In 1913, the Dr. Susan La Flesche Picotte Memorial Hospital opened on a hill above Walthill—one of the first hospitals in the United States built on Native land with privately raised funds rather than federal appropriations. The small Craftsman-style building held two general wards, five private rooms, a maternity ward, an operating room, a kitchen, bathrooms, and office space. For Susan, it was meant as more than a clinic; it was a statement that Omaha could build and control its own modern health institution.

Ironically, her health was deteriorating. She suffered from chronic ear and mastoid infections and what most historians now believe was bone cancer affecting her spine and skull, causing intense pain. Despite this, she continued to see patients, oversee the hospital's early operations, and serve as pastor to a local Presbyterian congregation in the Omaha language.

Final Years and Legacy

On September 18, 1915, Susan died in Walthill at age fifty. Her hospital remained in use into the 1940s, later serving as a care facility for elders and, in more recent years, becoming the Dr. Susan La Flesche Picotte Center, a community space and historic site honoring her life. Her former house has been listed on the National Register of Historic Places, and statues and educational programs across Nebraska and beyond now recognize her as a pioneer not only for Native people but also for women in medicine overall.

I shall always fight good and hard even if I have to fight alone.

Susan La Flesche Picotte, M.D.

(Library of Congress/Carol M. Highsmith)

Ben Victor's bronze sculpture of Dr. Susan La Flesche Picotte stands on Centennial Mall in Lincoln, Nebraska. (Library of Congress/Carol M. Highsmith)

Yet the record she left—letters to Washington, reports to church boards, careful descriptions of Omaha gardens, beliefs, and daily struggles—is as important as the "firsts" attached to her name. Susan La Flesche Picotte used the tools of a white professional world—degrees, medical charts, official correspondence—to argue that her people were neither relics nor wards, but modern citizens whose survival depended on clean water, secure land, sober law, and care delivered in their own language. In the quiet heroism of those long rides between agency and farmhouse, hospital and hearing room, the cultural collision of her era becomes concrete: policy turned into pain, and, through her work, into something closer to healing.

---

[1] Valerie Mathes, "Susan LaFlesche Picotte, M.D.: Nineteenth-Century Physician and Reformer," Great Plains Quarterly 13, no. 3 (1993): 172–186.

[2] Joseph Agonito, Brave Hearts: Indian Women of the Plains (Lanham, MD: Rowman & Littlefield, 2016), 159.

Chapter 8— Olive Oatman: The Blue-Tattooed Survivor Who Lived With The Mohave

"I walk forward because my heart tells me there is a future."

—Pretty Shield, Crow Medicine Woman

OLIVE OATMAN'S STORY BEGINS as a familiar tale of a pioneer family heading west. It becomes something far stranger: a girl marked for life by the blue tattoo of another people, standing uneasily between two worlds that both try to claim her. Her years with the Mohave, and the way that experience was later retold, say as much about white America's fears and fantasies as they do about the actual life she lived along the Colorado River.

The Oatman Massacre

In late 1850, Roys and Mary Ann Oatman left Illinois with their seven children, part of a Mormon splinter group heading to California for a fresh start. The children ranged in age from one to seventeen, with Lucy Oatman the eldest. Mary Ann was eight months pregnant with their eighth child.

Bound for the so-called "Land of Bashan," they joined a Brewsterite wagon train that departed from Independence, Missouri, in August. Roys Oatman was difficult and quarrelsome, and other members of the party began distancing themselves from him and his family as they traveled along the Santa Fé Trail through Kansas, New Mexico, the northern reaches of the Mexican state of Sonora, and what would soon become southern Arizona. By February, as they followed the Gila River, they made a fateful decision.

When the wagon train they'd been traveling with stopped near a friendly Pima village to rest and resupply, Roys insisted on pushing ahead alone with his family. Four days out from Maricopa Wells, a group of nineteen Native Americans, most likely Western Yavapai, approached them and asked for tobacco and food.

Roys shared a little bread but refused to give more, fearing for his family's supply in a desert already strained by drought. The visitors grew angry. Within moments, they attacked with clubs, killing Roys, Mary Ann, and four of the children.

Fifteen-year-old Lorenzo was beaten and left among the bodies. When he regained consciousness, there was no sign of Mary Ann or Olive. He began the trek to find help. Three days later, he returned to his slain family's bodies and began a years-long search for his sisters.

Olive and Mary Ann had been taken by the attackers and forced north into the rugged country of central Arizona as slaves.

Among the Yavapai

The first year of the girls' captivity was harsh. Later accounts, based on Olive's testimony and local records, describe them doing hard work, collecting firewood, carrying water, grinding food, all under the close watch of their captors. Food was scarce during a severe drought, and the Yavapai camp itself barely avoided starving. Olive would later highlight their suffering during this time and said she believed they would be killed, a view that matched what eastern audiences expected from a "savage captivity" story.

Oatman Massacre, Captivity of the Oatman Girls by Royal B. Stratton. Used for Educational Purposes

Sometime in 1852, a Mohave party visiting the Yavapai on a trading trip took notice of the two thin, overworked Anglo sisters. According to both Mohave oral history and later interviews, the daughter of a Mohave leader, known to Americans as Espaniole, saw the girls' condition and pressed her father to acquire them. After at least one refusal, the Yavapai agreed to trade: for two horses, some vegetables, blankets, and beads, the Oatman girls passed into Mohave hands.

Adoption by the Mohave

The journey to the Mohave village along the Colorado River, near what is now Needles, California, took several days on foot. When the sisters arrived, they were brought into the household of Espaniole and his wife, Aespaneo, who would become central figures in Olive's life.

Unlike the lean Yavapai camp, the Mohave community along the river was relatively prosperous, with irrigated fields of corn, beans, and squash. Aespaneo and her daughter, Topeka, took an immediate interest in the girls' welfare, giving them plots of land to farm and ensuring they were fed. Years later, Olive repeatedly expressed deep affection for these two women, remembering them as protectors rather than tormentors.

Evidence from Mohave oral traditions and anthropological work suggests that Olive was fully adopted. She was called by a Mohave name, "Oach," and was given a nickname, "Spantsa." Most importantly, received the distinctive blue tattoo on her chin (and possibly arms) that marked her as a member of the tribe. Olive would later tell lecture audiences that the tattoo was to brand her as a slave; however, Mohave practice belies that claim: such tattoos were reserved for community members so that, in the land of the dead, their ancestors would recognize them as Mohave.

This is one of the core tensions in her story. In public, Olive framed her Mohave years as a long captivity. Yet her actions at the time tell a more complicated tale: when a party of white railroad surveyors camped near the Mohave village for nearly a week in 1854, trading and socializing, she did not reveal herself to them. She knew white people were near, but she stayed with her adopted family.[1]

Famine and Loss

Life along the Colorado wasn't always idyllic. Sometime around 1854–1855, a severe drought hit the region, destroying crops and increasing hunger in the village. The Mohave rationed their food; some families endured long periods without. Olive and Mary Ann, who had less physical resilience than those born to the climate, suffered just as everyone else did.

Mary Ann, always frailer than her older sister, began to decline. Olive later said that her younger sister died of starvation during this drought, a claim supported by both local records and Mohave tradition. Her death left Olive alone among the Mohave, the last surviving daughter of the wagon that had rolled into the Arizona desert four years earlier.

By this point, Olive spoke the language, worked her own fields, and moved through daily life as one of the people around her. According to later accounts, she was allowed to leave for the white settlements whenever she chose, but the Mohave were wary of taking her themselves, concerned about having kept a white woman for so long.

Olive believed her brother Lorenzo had died in the massacre, and with her parents and siblings gone, the Mohave were, in practical terms, her only family.

Return to the Americans

One day, when Olive was 19, a Yuma Indian messenger arrived in the village. He carried a message from the authorities at Fort Yuma, a U.S. Army post on the lower Colorado. News of a "white woman with a blue tattoo" living among the Mohave had reached them, and the post commander requested her return or an explanation for why she had not returned.

The Mohaves initially refused, even denying that Olive was white. During negotiations, some showed affection for Oatman, while others expressed fear of retribution from whites. A second effort to persuade the Mohaves to give up Oatman was made, this time including trade items such as blankets and a white horse, along with threats that violence could erupt if she was not returned.

After some discussion, this time including Olive, the terms were accepted, and she was escorted to Fort Yuma on a 20-day journey. Topeka, the daughter of Espianola and Aespaneo, accompanied her.[2]

In early spring of 1856, Olive arrived at the fort wearing only a Mohave skirt, with her chin tattoo clearly visible. Before entering, she was given Western clothing borrowed from an army officer's wife and was greeted by cheering crowds. Within days, she learned that Lorenzo had survived the 1851 attack and had been searching for her and Mary Ann for several years. Their tearful reunion soon made headlines; newspapers across the West ran dramatic stories of the "white girl rescued from savages," often viewing her blue tattoo with both horror and fascination.

Fort Yuma, accessed December 2025
https://www.army.mil/article/75695/fort_yuma_critical_to_westward_e
xpansion_in_frontier_days

The story she shared publicly, however, was not entirely
her own. A Methodist minister named Royal Byron Stratton
convinced Olive and Lorenzo to allow him to write their
story. The result, published in 1857 as "Captivity of the
Oatman Girls," followed the familiar pattern of
Indian-captivity narratives that highlight suffering,
"savagery," and miraculous rescue, while minimizing
affection, adoption, or personal agency. It sold widely, and
the royalties helped fund both siblings' education at the
University of the Pacific.

At Stratton's side, Olive went on a lecture circuit, standing
on stages from New York to the Midwest, retelling her

ordeal for paying audiences. She wore long sleeves to hide the tattoos on her arms. The one on her chin, impossible to conceal completely, became the visual hook of every broadsheet and advertisement.

For white Americans of the 1850s, Olive's blue tattoo was proof that she had been "marked" by the other side of the frontier, a visible sign that the line between "us" and "them" could be crossed and, perhaps, never entirely erased.

Yet small cracks in that public story remained. Years after her return, she spoke fondly of "old times" with Irataba, a Mohave leader she had met in New York. The meeting suggests genuine attachment beneath the rhetoric. Her nickname among the Mohave, remembered in tribal memory, and the fact that she had not tried to run to earlier white visitors point to someone who had once felt truly at home on the Colorado.

Later Years

In 1864, while lecturing in Michigan, Olive met a New York–born cattleman and rancher named John Brant Fairchild. They married in Rochester, New York, in 1865, and she left the stage behind. After a period in the Midwest, the couple settled in Sherman, Texas, where Fairchild founded the City Bank and prospered in banking and real estate.

In Sherman, Olive tried to disappear into respectability. She and John moved into a large Victorian house, adopted a baby girl they named Mary Elizabeth, and devoted themselves to local charities, especially an orphanage.

Olive began wearing veils or heavy cosmetics to hide the tattoo that had made her famous, and Fairchild quietly bought up copies of Stratton's book and burned them when he could find them.

Olive Oatman Fairchild

Those close to her described a woman plagued by depression and chronic headaches, often reluctant to leave her home. She died in 1903 at age sixty-five and was buried in Sherman, far from the desert mesa where her family fell and the river valley where she once farmed as a Mohave woman.

The Story and the Woman

Olive Oatman's life was shaped as much by other people's stories as by her own choices. The massacre, the Yavapai year, the Mohave adoption, the blue tattoo, and the reunion at Fort Yuma all happened in the narrow space where cultures clashed across the Southwest.

What came after, the lecture circuit, the sensational book, and years spent behind a veil in Texas, demonstrates how a single frontier life could be claimed, revised, and retold until the woman at its center almost disappeared behind the legend.

Yet certain facts endure. A Mohave household took her in, fed her, and marked her as one of their own. She buried a sister in Colorado and never saw that land again. She carried a blue tattoo to her grave that meant two very different things, depending on who was looking at it. And in that tension between mark and meaning lies the deeper story: the story of a frontier where identity, once crossed, could never be entirely walked back.

[1] Oatman Massacre Collection, Yuma County Library District.
[2] R. B. Stratton, Captivity of the Oatman Girls: Being an Interesting Narrative of Life Among the Apache and Mohave Indians (New York: Miller, Orton & Mulligan, 1857).

Chapter 9 — Sarah Winnemucca: Northern Paiute Diplomat, Interpreter, and Author

"I was a very small child when the first white people came into our country. They came like a lion, yes, like a roaring lion, and have continued so ever since, and I have never forgotten their first coming."

— Sarah Winnemucca

SARAH WINNEMUCCA SPOKE FOR herself in a way few Native women of the 19th century were allowed to do, using English, print, and the lecture stage to insist that the story of westward expansion also included the voices and rights of the Northern Paiute. Born into a world already under pressure from miners, settlers, and federal agents, she tried to stand between her people and the United States, translating not only words but entire ways of thinking.

Early Life on Paiute Land

Sarah, the granddaughter of Chief Truckee, known as "Thocmetony" (Shell Flower), was born around 1844 near the Humboldt River in present-day Nevada. Her family was an influential Northern Paiute family that worked to maintain peaceful relations with incoming Anglo-American settlers. She was the daughter of Chief Winnemucca of the Paiute.[1]

As a child, she traveled with her family through northern Nevada, living a seasonal, mobile life of fishing, hunting, and gathering seeds in a landscape her people had used for generations.

During this period, the Paiutes' way of life in the Great Basin changed significantly. Sudden migration occurred after gold was discovered in California and silver at the Comstock Lode in Nevada, replacing their earlier sporadic contact with Spanish officials and American traders. Now, wagon roads, mining camps, and ranches steadily intruded on the land.

Early Nevada

Her grandfather, Truckee, had a notably friendly attitude toward newcomers and even worked for John C. Frémont as a guide during his 1843–45 expedition across the Great Basin to California. Truckee believed in promoting peaceful relations and hoped that coexistence could protect his people. Sarah's early memories, later written down, captured both this effort at friendship and the shock of violence that erupted when settlers and Paiutes clashed.

California

When she was six years old, the family began working in the cattle industry and moved to Stockton, California. In 1857, when she was 13, Sarah and her sister Elma were sent to live and work in the household of a Carson City hotel owner, William. Ormsby and his wife wanted a companion for their daughter, Lizzie.

The Winnemucca girls also did housework, improved their English, and learned more about European-American customs. Sarah eventually felt comfortable moving between the two cultures and was one of the few Paiute who could read and write in both English and Spanish. She also adopted the English name Sarah.

War, Loss, and Interpreting

With the declining influx of new migrants in Nevada, Old Winnemucca arranged in 1859 to have his daughters brought back to him.

When Sarah was 16, tensions at Pyramid Lake escalated into war after local settlers' attacks on Paiute families prompted retaliation. The large U.S. military response that followed forced many Northern Paiutes onto a reservation at Pyramid Lake, where they faced shortages of promised rations and lost their traditional hunting and gathering lands. Many Paiute died of starvation. After Sarah intervened and asked for food, military officials at Camp McDermit (later Fort McDermit) finally sent rations.

From 1860 to 1865, Sarah and her family began telling their story directly to white audiences; the Winnemuccas toured as a small theatrical troupe. They spent long stretches in the booming mining town of Virginia City, Nevada, and in San Francisco, renting hall space and performing at venues such as Maguire's Opera House.

Advertised to non-Native crowds as "A Paiute Royal Family," they earned their living by allowing audiences to see what they imagined as "Indian royalty," even though Paiute political life had no kings, queens, or princesses in the European sense.

Contemporary descriptions and later scholarship suggest that these performances combined costumed "traditional" displays with spoken addresses in English. Sarah already spoke fluent English and Spanish, and she used that skill onstage.

While her father and relatives embodied the crowd's expectations of "real Indians," Sarah functioned as cultural mediator, greeting audiences in polished English and explaining Paiute grievances and needs in terms white spectators could understand. Historians have pointed out that the "royal" and "princess" language attached to her stage persona was a white invention that both distorted Paiute social structures and gave Sarah a kind of public authority she could turn toward advocacy for her people.

The Winnemuccas' theatrical work unfolded amid escalating violence. In March 1865, while Sarah and her

106

father were away, the Nevada Volunteer Cavalry attacked their band's camp at Mud Lake (later called Winnemucca Lake), killing twenty-nine Paiute people, almost all women, children, and elders. Among the dead were Sarah's mother, Tuboitonie, and a baby brother; one sister escaped on horseback and was the only survivor.

Sarah later described the attack, known as the Mud Lake Massacre, in her autobiography, insisting that "it must be told" even though, as she wrote, the telling was "a fearful thing."

The contrast was stark: while white audiences applauded the so-called "Paiute Royal Family" under the gaslights of Virginia City and San Francisco, Sarah's actual relatives were being killed in the desert interior. Those five years on stage were not a romantic interlude but a survival strategy shaped by war, famine, and state violence.

Sarah's linguistic abilities—including Northern Paiute, English, and some Spanish—placed her at the center of these upheavals. In 1871, at about twenty-seven, she became an interpreter for the Bureau of Indian Affairs at Fort McDermitt and later at the Malheur Reservation. There, she helped teach Paiute communities to plant crops that could sustain them, contributing to a more successful agricultural program. A school was established on the reservation, where Sarah served as an assistant teacher.

The Malheur Reservation in eastern Oregon, established in 1872, was designated by President Ulysses S. Grant for the Northern Paiute and Bannock peoples in the area. Three bands of Paiute moved there at the time. In 1875,

Winnemucca, her brother Natchez, his family, and their father, Old Winnemucca, also moved there.

Bannock War

When William V. Rinehart, a new Bureau of Indian Affairs agent, was appointed in 1876, policies that had once benefited the Paiute were reversed. An advocate of extermination-style warfare, Rinehart focused on asserting control over the Paiute. He withheld payment for their labor, alienating many tribal leaders. Conditions at the Malheur Reservation quickly became intolerable.

In her 1883 book, Sarah later wrote that Rinehart sold supplies meant for the Paiute to local whites and that much of the reservation's most valuable land was being illegally seized by white settlers. In 1878, nearly all of the Paiute and Bannock left the reservation because of the harsh conditions they faced. The Bannock from southern Idaho had already departed the Fort Hall Reservation over similar grievances. Moving west, they raided small white settlements in southern Oregon and northern Nevada, culminating in the Bannock War of 1878.

It is unclear how much the Northern Paiute people participated with the Bannock. Sarah later wrote that many Paiute families were pressured by the Bannock to support them.

It was during this time that Sarah worked as a translator for the U.S. Army and served as a scout and messenger, encouraging Northern Paiute bands to cooperate in hopes of avoiding harsher treatment. This role later caused some of her own people to view her as being too close to the Army.[2]

Unlike most Indian reformers of her era, Sarah trusted the US soldiers she collaborated with. However, she did not hesitate to criticize the hypocrisy of the Indian Office agents, who used Christian benevolence to justify violence and the removal of Indians. She wrote:

"Oh, for shame!...Yes, you, who call yourselves the great civilization; you who have knelt upon Plymouth Rock, covenanting with God to make this land the home of the free and the brave. Ah, then you rise from your bended knees and seizing the welcoming hands of those who are the owners of this land, which you are not, your carbines rise upon the bleak shore, and your so-called civilization sweeps in land from the ocean wave; but, oh, my God! leaving its pathway marked by crimson lines of blood, and strewed by the bones of two races, the inheritor and the invader; and I am crying out to you for justice."[3]

Malheur, Yakama, and Betrayal

After the Bannock War, conditions on the Malheur reservation deteriorated even more. Rations were withheld or stolen, and Paiute families faced starvation despite their labor. Sarah used her role as an interpreter to speak out, translating complaints in meetings and writing letters for her people, which led to her dismissal from the agency.

The federal government imposed its punishment on the Paiutes by forcing many of them to march hundreds of miles in winter from Malheur to the Yakama Reservation in Washington Territory. Conditions there were poor, with inadequate shelter and food. The Northern Paiute blamed both the government and, in some cases, the compromises Sarah had urged in hopes of avoiding worse.

Sarah "Thocmetony" Winnemucca

Sarah was devastated by the removal and by the accusations of betrayal. Rather than withdraw, she escalated her activism, deciding that if local agents and officers would not listen, she would take her case to the national stage.

Life Among the Paiutes

In 1880, Sarah traveled to Washington, D.C., with her father and other leaders to advocate for the Paiutes' right to return to Malheur; she met with the Secretary of the Interior and received written permission, which local authorities at Yakama later refused to honor. Recognizing she needed broader public support, she began giving lectures in San Francisco and then across the eastern United States, delivering over 300 talks between 1883 and 1884. She also taught at Fort Vancouver and the Peabody Institute in Lovelock, Nevada.

In 1883, Sarah turned her lectures into a book titled *Life Among the Paiutes: Their Wrongs and Claims*. The work combines autobiography, tribal history, and political argument, recounting early encounters with settlers, broken treaties, massacres, and the suffering at Malheur and Yakama. It concludes with a petition urging readers to support the restoration of Paiute homelands and rights. Scholars have described it as the first known autobiography by a Native American woman and one of the earliest ethnohistorical works by an Indigenous author.

Sarah crafted her English prose for the reform audiences of her time, blending biblical allusions and sentimental scenes with sharp factual claims about hunger, theft, and official corruption. Simultaneously, she included Paiute oral stories and origin legends to emphasize that her people's connection to the land and their moral principles existed before and outlasted U.S. expansion.

Teacher, Organizer, and Legacy

After the book's publication, Sarah returned west and tried to build the kind of just community she imagined. In 1885, she established a private school for Paiute children near Lovelock, Nevada, hoping to offer education under Native control rather than through distant reservation boarding schools. Chronic lack of funding and political support forced the school to close after a few years, a pattern that echoed her larger battles with federal policy.

She spent her final years moving between Native communities and white towns, still writing letters, visiting officials, and speaking whenever she could, even as her health declined. Sarah Winnemucca died in October 1891 near Monida, Montana, while staying with relatives; she was in her forties.

Today, her work continues to influence both historians and Native activists. *Life Among the Piutes* remains a key primary source for the early reservation era in the Great Basin and a rare 19th-century Native woman's voice addressing the U.S. public directly. Statues, state honors, and scholarly studies now name her as an educator, diplomat, and "newspaper warrior." Still, the core of her legacy is simpler: she insisted that the Northern Paiute were not obstacles to a frontier, but a nation with history, rights, and a story they could tell themselves.

Sarah "Thocmetony" Winnemucca

[1] "Sarah Winnemucca," National Park Service
[2] Sarah Winnemucca Hopkins, Life Among the Piutes: Their Wrongs and Claims (Boston: Cupples, Upham & Co., 1883), 207.
[3] "Sarah Winnemucca," Journal of California and Great Basin Anthropology 5, no. 2 (1983).

Part III — Courage, Conflict, and Cause:
Women Who Shaped Frontier Politics,
Justice, and War

Chapter 10 — Susannah Dickinson: The Alamo Survivor

"The frontier was not a place, but a way of seeing."

— Mari Sandoz

SUSANNA DICKINSON'S STORY BEGINS not with the thunder of cannon at the Alamo, but with a young, nearly illiterate Tennessee woman swept into the upheaval of the Texas Revolution, and then, almost by accident, into history. When virtually every defender inside the Alamo died on March 6, 1836, she and her baby daughter walked out alive, carrying a message that would send Sam Houston and the Texian army into a desperate retreat and, eventually, a final stand at San Jacinto.

Into the Alamo

Susanna Wilkerson was born around 1814, probably in Williamson County, Tennessee, and by her late teens, she had little formal schooling and few prospects beyond marriage. In 1829, at about age fifteen, she married Almaron Dickinson, a gunsmith and militia man, and they followed the wave of Anglo settlers into Mexican Texas, first to the Gonzales area and later to San Antonio de Béxar.[1]

By October 1835, tensions between Mexican authorities and Texian settlers had erupted into open conflict, and the couple fled to San Antonio, where Texian forces had occupied the former mission of San Antonio de Valero, the Alamo.

The Alamo

On February 23, as Santa Anna's army arrived in San Antonio and church bells sounded the alarm, Almaron rode to their small house in town, seized their infant daughter Angelina, and shouted for Susanna to mount behind him. They crossed the San Antonio River under fire and entered the Alamo just as Mexican troops were pouring into the city, beginning the thirteen-day siege.

There was no food inside to sustain them during the siege. Cattle were quickly herded, and food was sought in nearby abandoned houses.

The Alamo, Public Domain

Meanwhile, Susanna cooked, washed, and cared for baby Angelina in cramped quarters while cannon and small arms fire battered the compound. She later recalled becoming familiar with the leading figures: James Bowie, who was dangerously ill; William Barret Travis, writing his doomed appeals for reinforcements; and David Crockett, whose fiddle and Tennessee stories were a brief relief from the constant fear.[2]

Dawn, March 6

The bombardments stopped around nightfall on March 5, lulling exhausted defenders into their first uninterrupted sleep since the siege began, just as Santa Anna planned.

At pre-dawn on March 6th, Santa Anna ordered the final assault. Under the cover of darkness, Mexican columns advanced with scaling ladders, then swarmed the walls just as the sky began to lighten.

Almaron Dickinson was manning a cannon when, early in the assault, he ran to the chapel where Susanna was sheltering with Angelina and other noncombatants. He cried, "Great God, Sue, the Mexicans are inside our walls! If they spare you, save my child!", then kissed her and returned to his post. She never saw him again. Before taking his assigned position, she recalled Davy Crockett stopping to pray.[3]

Susanna's view of the battle was limited; she later admitted she did not see the fighting in the courtyards and barracks firsthand. She heard the shouting, pounding, splintering wood, and screams. At least one Texian defender burst into her hiding spot, trying to hide, only to be killed in front of her by Mexican soldiers.

When the gunfire finally ceased, the Alamo's interior was filled with bodies—nearly 190 Texian defenders and hundreds of Mexican soldiers, including Almaron, who operated the two 12-pounder cannons in the chapel. They had fired their cannon at the Mexican soldiers and had no time to reload. Dickinson, Gregorio Esparza, Bonham, and the remaining Texians seized their rifles and returned fire, but they were overwhelmed and bayoneted.

Master of the Ordinance, Texian Robert Evans, was tasked with preventing the Mexicans from obtaining the gunpowder. Wounded, he crawled toward the powder magazine when a musket ball struck him just short of his goal. His torch fell only inches from the gunpowder; had he succeeded, the resulting explosion would have destroyed the chapel, killing everyone inside, including Susanna and the other women and children sheltering there.[4]

It was in the ruined church that Susanna was hiding with little Angelina and other noncombatants.

In later accounts, she said that, after the gunfire slackened, she heard a Mexican soldier calling her name and realized the fort had fallen. With Angelina in her arms, she stepped out from the shelter of the chapel and followed several soldiers as they led the survivors away through smoke and rubble. On the way out, she was struck in the leg by a bullet, whether by accident or design, she never knew. The wound never fully healed and troubled her for the rest of her life.

Susanna told interviewers that when soldiers leveled weapons toward her, a Mexican officer intervened and ordered that she and the baby be spared. In some retellings, that rescuer is remembered simply as "a Mexican soldier";

later writers have suggested he may have been Colonel Juan Nepomuceno Almonte or an English volunteer known as "Black." Whatever his exact identity, Susanna walked out of the Alamo alive, Angelina in her arms, and was taken with the other women and children to the nearby Músquiz home in San Antonio.

From there, she was brought before Santa Anna, who questioned her about the garrison, their numbers, and their actions. Some later accounts say he offered to take Angelina to Mexico for her upbringing and education; Susanna refused. Before releasing them, he gave each a blanket and two silver dollars, gestures meant as a gesture of generosity from a victor. Then he ordered the defenders' bodies burned in mass pyres outside the walls.

Then she was chosen to carry a warning and the news of the Alamo's destruction to Sam Houston.

Messenger of the Alamo

On March 7 or 8, Mexican officers selected Susanna and her child, along with two other survivors, to serve as living warnings. She was given a letter and instructed to tell Houston that if the rebels continued to resist, they would face the same fate as the men at the Alamo.

The journey east was difficult. Traveling on a mule and guarded by a Mexican officer's servant, Susanna passed through smoldering ruins and past refugees fleeing Santa Anna's army. Near Gonzales, she met other Texian scouts who guided her the rest of the way to Houston's camp on the Colorado. Later, she remembered that she wept for days.

Painting of Susanna Dickinson leaving the Alamo by Harry Anthony De Young, 1941.

On March 13–15, 1836, Houston wrote several letters mentioning the fall of the Alamo, saying that "the wife of Lieutenant Dickinson…confirms the fall of that place, and the circumstances, pretty much as my express detailed them." Susanna's physical presence, as an eyewitness, widowed, and carrying a baby, did what written reports could not: it made the disaster real.

Houston responded by ordering a strategic retreat eastward, the "Runaway Scrape," buying time until he could fight on ground of his choosing at San Jacinto in April.

From that point forward, in Texas memory, Susanna became "the Messenger of the Alamo."

Hard Years on the Frontier

The years following her sudden rise to fame were anything but easy. Widowed around twenty-two, almost illiterate, and traumatized, Susanna went through a series of unstable relationships and financial hardships.

In December 1838, she married Francis P. Herring, who died just five years later, leaving her once again with little support. In 1847, she married a drayman named Peter Bellows, but by 1854, she had left him; in later divorce papers, he accused her of adultery and claimed she had lived in a "house of ill fame." Meanwhile, other contemporaries noted that she cared for cholera victims during epidemics in Houston, demonstrating a woman trying, despite difficult circumstances, to survive respectably on a rough frontier.

Susanna also used her Alamo experience to help others. On several occasions, she testified for widows and heirs of Alamo defenders seeking land grants from the Republic and later the State of Texas. Her statements about who had died at the mission carried both legal and moral significance. She recounted the battle many times over the years, with her last known account given shortly before her death in 1883, later published in the memoirs of fellow Texan Mary Maverick.[5]

A Final Home in Austin

Stability and contentment came late. In 1857, in the town of Lockhart, she met a German immigrant cabinetmaker, Joseph William Hannig. They married that same year and moved to Austin, where Hannig built a prosperous cabinet shop, furniture store, and undertaking business. In 1869, he constructed a handsome limestone home on East 5th Street; the couple lived there for the rest of Susanna's life.

By the 1870s, visitors described her as living quietly in this "beautiful home," no longer a transient widow but the respected wife of a prosperous merchant. Yet the Alamo never entirely left her. Historian Stephen Hardin and others note that even late in life, she vividly recalled the piles of bodies, the smoke, the screams, and the moment she was spared when she walked out of the rubble with Angelina in her arms.

Susanna fell ill in early 1883 and died in Austin on October 7 of that year. She was buried in Oakwood Cemetery. Her Austin home is now a museum, dedicated to the woman whose survival linked two defining scenes of the Texas Revolution: the fall of the Alamo and the decision to fight on.

In public memory, Susanna Dickinson is often reduced to a single image: a young woman stepping out of the smoke with a baby on her hip. The full story is more complex: a life shaped by trauma, poverty, gossip, work, multiple marriages, and late-won security. Yet that single moment remains historically pivotal: without her living testimony, carried east from a destroyed mission to a cautious general, the course of the Texas Revolution—and the story of the American Southwest—might have turned out differently.

Susanna Dickinson

[1] King, C. Richard (1976). Susanna Dickinson: messenger of the Alamo (1st ed.). Austin, Tex: Shoal Creek Publishers. pp. 2–4.
[2] Nofi, The Alamo and the Texas War of Independence, p. 139
[3] Edmondson, J.R. (2000), The Alamo Story-From History to Current Conflicts, Plano, TX: Republic of Texas Press
[4] Petite, Mary Deborah (1999), 1836 Facts about the Alamo and the Texas War for Independence, Mason City, IA: Savas Publishing
[5] Nofi, Albert A. (1992), The Alamo and the Texas War of Independence, September 30, 1835 to April 21, 1836: Heroes, Myths, and History, Conshohocken, PA: Combined Books, Inc.

Chapter 11— Delia Ann Webster: The Underground Railroad Operative Who Defied Slavery

"A woman's work is never small when the land is wide."

—Lucy Thompson (C'olek'uhl)

DELIA ANN WEBSTER STEPPED into the fight against slavery not with a rifle or a speech in Congress, but with a rented carriage, a Vermont education, and a willingness to stare down the slave power on its own ground. In 1844, she helped spirit a family out of Lexington, Kentucky, into freedom and paid for it with a prison term that made her one of the first women in the United States jailed for work on the Underground Railroad.

From Vermont to the Borderland

Delia Webster was born on December 17, 1817, in rural Vergennes, Vermont, into a humble farming family that valued education enough to send her to local academies. By the mid-1830s, she was teaching school, and a few years later, she briefly enrolled at Oberlin College in Ohio, the first U.S. college to admit both Black students and women. Oberlin was a hub of abolitionism; antislavery speakers, petitions, and rumors of "Underground Railroad" activity were part of daily life.

By 1843–1844, Delia had taken a post in Lexington, Kentucky, where she taught at a female academy. Lexington was slave territory, but it was also threaded with quiet antislavery networks reaching across the Ohio River, which was only a day's journey away. Through contacts there and in Ohio, Delia connected with the itinerant Methodist minister Calvin Fairbank, an abolitionist based in Ohio who had already helped dozens of enslaved people escape north.

The Hayden Escape

In Lexington, Delia and Fairbank met Lewis Hayden, a literate, skilled enslaved man who worked in a clothing store and was owned, along with his wife, Harriet, and young son, Joseph, by a local merchant. Hayden had long dreamed of freedom. When Fairbank asked why he wanted to escape, Hayden answered simply: "Because I am a man."

On September 28, 1844, the plan went into motion. Fairbank rented a horse and carriage; Delia left her lodgings and joined him and the Hayden family on the road out of Lexington. To disguise themselves, Lewis and Harriet dusted their faces with flour to appear white or at least less conspicuous; little Joseph hid under the carriage seat. They rode northeast toward Maysville, Kentucky, and the Ohio River, intending to cross into the free state and then move on by Underground Railroad stations to the well-known abolitionist safe house of Reverend John Rankin and ultimately to Canada.

The immediate escape was successful. The Haydens crossed the river into Ohio, eventually settling in Boston, where Lewis became a prominent abolitionist and later joined the Massachusetts legislature. However, Kentucky authorities quickly traced the help back to the white conspirators. As Delia and Fairbank were returning to Lexington, slaveholders raised the alarm; both were arrested and imprisoned, charged with "aiding and enticing slaves to escape," commonly called "slave stealing."

"The Underground Railroad," painted by Charles Webster in 1893, depicts what was likely a common scene along the fugitive network— courtesy of the Library of Congress.

Trial and Imprisonment

The trials in late 1844 drew intense attention in Lexington and beyond. While Fairbank was viewed as the primary operative, much of the documentary evidence, including letters from abolitionists and notes about routes, was found in Delia's rented room after her landlady searched it and handed materials to authorities. Their lawyers managed to secure separate trials; public sympathy inclined more to Delia, a young, unmarried white woman, than to the outspoken male minister who had already earned a reputation as a "slave thief."

Despite her plea of not guilty, the all-male jury convicted her. In December 1844, she was sentenced to two years' hard labor in the Kentucky State Penitentiary at Frankfort, the first woman in the state imprisoned for Underground Railroad activity and, by most accounts, one of the first in the nation. Fairbank, tried separately, received fifteen years, five for each enslaved person he had helped in the Hayden case.[1]

On January 10, 1845, Delia entered the penitentiary. Because she was the only female prisoner, officials lodged her in a small wooden cottage in the prison yard rather than the main cell blocks. Crowds gathered outside the walls; newspapers in Kentucky and the North reported on "Miss Webster," debating whether a woman should be subjected to prison for helping enslaved people flee. Within weeks, jurors from her own trial signed a petition asking the governor to show mercy, explicitly "on account of her sex."

Public pressure worked. On February 24, 1845, after just about five weeks, Governor John J. Crittenden issued her a full pardon, reportedly after she agreed to issue a statement softening or renouncing her abolitionist beliefs. Fairbank, by contrast, remained in prison for years, subjected to whippings and hard labor that left him permanently damaged.

The Petticoat Abolitionist

If Kentucky hoped prison would silence her, it misjudged Delia Webster.

Back in Vermont, she published a pamphlet almost immediately: *Kentucky Jurisprudence: A History of the Trial of Miss Delia A. Webster*, an account of her arrest, trial, and imprisonment framed as an indictment of pro-slavery law. She spoke at antislavery meetings, met leaders of the American Anti-Slavery Society in the Northeast, and used her brief notoriety to raise funds and contacts for further work.

By the early 1850s, she had moved to Madison, Indiana, a river town directly opposite Kentucky, and quietly resumed Underground Railroad work. Madison was a key crossing point; free Black and white abolitionists there ran boats and wagons across the Ohio under cover of night. Delia, now labeled in some newspapers as the "petticoat abolitionist," again put herself at risk in a border region where pro-slavery feeling ran strong.

Mount Orison: A Farm on the Line

In 1854, with money raised from Boston abolitionists and other supporters, Delia purchased a 600-acre farm along the Kentucky border. She called it "Mt. Orison" and envisioned it as both a working farm and a strategically placed station on the Underground Railroad, a place where fugitives could be hidden, fed, and then moved safely northward.

She hired free Black laborers and planned additional enterprises, including a mill and a shoe shop, to make the property economically viable and provide work for those she harbored. But her presence as a known abolitionist woman, operating a large farm in slaveholding Kentucky, immediately drew suspicion and hostility. Local slaveholders accused her of harboring their enslaved people and warned that she, her farm, or her workers might be harmed if she stayed.

A 1921 article in the *Indiana Magazine of History* described her abolitionist efforts: "She came to be hated by the slave masters as well as feared by them. She was constantly under suspicion and was subjected to threats intermingled with much persecution. With all this opposition, she continued her work just the same, traveling from one locality to another, always coming in contact with slaves and teaching them the avenues of escape and very frequently aiding them directly in the work herself."[2]

In 1854, whispers about "missing slaves" along the Kentucky border hardened into an arrest warrant for Delia Webster. Local slaveholders were sure she had helped them vanish, and the charge carried the full weight of the Fugitive Slave Act. Officers seized her and locked her in jail, but she slipped out—one of several escapes she would later hint at but never fully explain. She fled across the river to Madison, Indiana, moving from attic to barn to backwoods cabins as neighbors took turns hiding her. Posses crossed into the state, searching door to door. After weeks of pursuit, they closed in, and Webster was retaken—this time held under federal authority to await trial for aiding freedom seekers.[3]

That prosecution ended in a dismissed trial, but violence against her home and property worsened, and Delia repeatedly fled across the river to Indiana to avoid new indictments.

During the Civil War, she worked with Harriet Beecher Stowe on the Underground Railroad, and nursed wounded soldiers.[4]

In November 1866, her home was destroyed by arsonists, and, unable to continue financially, the property was foreclosed upon.

Later Years and Legacy

After the collapse of her Kentucky base, Delia moved through a series of Midwestern and New England towns, Cincinnati, Madison, and eventually Des Moines, Iowa, working as a teacher, artist, and sometimes land speculator. She never married, and her later life was marked by both poverty and legal property disputes. Still, she remained, in the words of one modern biographer, "strong-willed, independent, and unrepentant."

She died on January 18, 1904, in Des Moines, and was buried in a modest grave a long way from the Kentucky prison yard and the farm that had nearly cost her life.

In the larger memory of the Underground Railroad, Delia Webster's role is often overshadowed by figures like Harriet Tubman or Levi Coffin. Yet, her story reveals several key truths about that clandestine network. It depended not only on heroic escapes, but on white and Black allies embedded in hostile territory; on women willing to risk reputations, economic ruin, and prison; and on people who, like Delia, turned the tools of their time—education, pamphlets, property ownership—against a system that insisted they had no right to interfere.

As one Kentucky marker puts it, she is remembered as a woman who "after serving prison time…bought a farm overlooking the Ohio River…and continued her fight against slavery," a quiet line that does not quite capture the audacity of what that meant in the 1840s and 1850s American borderlands.

Delia Ann Webster

[1] James Lane Allen (1911). Aftermath, part second of "A Kentucky Cardinal". Macmillan Co. p. 70.

[2] George Streiby Cottman; Christopher Bush Coleman; Logan Esarey (1921). Indiana Magazine of History. p. 281. Retrieved 1 May 2013.

[3] George Streiby Cottman; Christopher Bush Coleman; Logan Esarey (1921). Indiana Magazine of History. pp. 283–286. Retrieved 1 May 2013.

[4] Michelle Arnosky Sherburne (August 6, 2013). Abolition & the Underground Railroad in Vermont. Arcadia Publishing Incorporated. pp. PT 105.

Chapter 12 — Eliza Farnham: Prison Reformer on a Gold Rush Frontier

"There's a land—oh, it beckons and beckons, and I want to go back—and I will."

— Robert W. Service

ELIZA FARNHAM'S LIFE RUNS like a thread through the institutions that defined 19th-century power: prisons, boomtowns, asylums, and battlefields. At each turn, she tried, in her own controversial way, to bend those places toward justice and toward women. From the women's ward at Sing Sing to a rough ranch in Gold Rush California, she asked one radical question for her time: what if punishment and frontier "progress" were judged by how they treated the most vulnerable, not the most powerful?

A Hard Childhood and a Radical Mind

Eliza Wood Burhans was born in 1815 in Rensselaerville, New York, to Cornelius and Mary Wood Burhans. After her mother died in 1820, five-year-old Eliza was sent to live with the Warrens, a childless couple, in a rural community in western New York State.

Her book My Early Days (1859) She describes her childhood as a period of constant suffering among ignorant, brutal people. Eliza worked as a servant for the Warrens, who were Quakers but openly atheistic. She recalled that she was not even called by her real name but by hostile nicknames, including "Tonewanta," a reference to her dark complexion.

Predominantly self-educated, Eliza loved books and nature. Those early years gave her a keen understanding of how authority could be misused within the home, a lesson she would later apply in her work in prisons.

By the late 1830s, she had married a restless lawyer and explorer, Thomas J. Farnham, and followed him west to Illinois and then back east again. They had two sons, Charles and Edward.

She began to write: first essays and then *Life in Prairie Land* (1846), a reflective account of frontier Illinois life that combined detailed observation with an emerging feminist consciousness. She was reading Elizabeth Fry, the great English Quaker prison reformer, and contemplating how women, as she expressed it, might be "superior" in moral perception and thus especially suited to reshape the institutions that punished society's failures.[1]

Matron of Sing Sing

In 1844, Eliza successfully applied to become matron of the women's division at the New York State Penitentiary at Sing Sing. The place had a dark local reputation of being riotous, filthy, and violent. There, women convicted of theft, assault, or prostitution were locked under a "silent system" that forbade speech and relied on isolation, hard labor, and beatings to enforce order.

Eliza came in determined to prove that "kindness was a more effective method of governance than brutality." Drawing on Fry's example, she enacted several reforms, including the end of strict silence, allowing women to speak during supervised work and instruction; she introduced a library of secular books and organized classes in reading, writing, history, and science; and she brought in music and religious services that emphasized hope rather than damnation.[2]

She also created a system of privileges and rewards to encourage self-control, instead of relying on physical punishment. She fought for better food and living conditions. Reports from sympathetic observers suggest that riots and overt violence in the women's wing declined under her tenure.

But her methods, especially her focus on secular reading and her unconventional spiritual views, angered the prison chaplain and conservative officials, who viewed her as "coddling" criminals and weakening religious authority. After a political shift in New York and several fierce confrontations with the chaplain, she was forced out in 1848; the new administration quickly reversed many of her reforms.

To California: Refinement in a Lawless Boomtown

Eliza's life took a sharp turn in 1848 when her husband died in California, leaving her land in Santa Cruz County and a complicated business in San Francisco. Instead of sending a male representative, she chose to go herself and, true to her character, turned necessity into a social experiment: she formed a small group of "respectable" unmarried women to accompany her and her children, hoping to "bring refinement to that disorderly city."

Early Sing Sing Prison

Their 1849 voyage around Cape Horn on the ship Angelique was chaotic. At one point, when Eliza went ashore in Chile to secure papers for a new servant, the captain sailed without her, taking her children and belongings onward. It was an early reminder that, even for a determined reformer, a woman's control over travel and property on the frontier could vanish in an instant.

Eliza waited in Chile for almost two months for another ship and finally arrived in San Francisco in February 1850. The city was a boomtown filled with gamblers, miners, and speculators who crowded the untamed streets. Men stared or jeered at her as she walked with her children. From there, along with her children and her baggage, Eliza ultimately made her way to Santa Cruz, where she took ownership of the 200-acre ranch that Thomas Farnham had left her, naming it El Rancho La Libertad.

The house was a slab-walled shack leaning at odd angles, barely weather-tight. Without a husband and little hired help, she set about making it livable: struggling for days to get a stubborn iron stove working, rebuilding walls, and overseeing farm work.

In 1851, Georgiana Bruce, Eliza's friend and former assistant at Sing Sing, moved in with her and her sons. She was again hopeful, writing: "We are going to be very independent and free… dashing about at our discretion."

The women roofed and joined the house, broke sod and set out potatoes, planted fruit trees, and raised chickens. To work and move freely, they wore bloomers instead of skirts, which was an amusing sight to the locals.

In 1856, she published *In-doors and Out*, the first book about California life written by a woman.

She depicted early gold camps, drunken Sabbath revelry, boy miners quickly learning vice alongside the skills of washing gold, and the hard labor of women trying to keep households afloat amid a male-dominated chaos. She commended miners' industry but also criticized their "drunkenness, carousing, and profanity," asserting that true manhood demanded restraint and a responsibility to families and the community.

She attempted once more to reshape frontier society by involving women at its center, encouraging organized female immigration to California.

The Invisible Architecture of Civilization

Women like Eliza understood something fundamental: the West wasn't just being settled by agriculture and mining. It was being civilized by the services and structures that made daily life possible—laundries, boarding houses, restaurants, schools, and medical care. Women dominated these enterprises, thereby shaping the economic landscape of frontier towns.

Eliza briefly remarried in 1852. Her youngest son, Eddie, died in 1855, and a year afterward, she left the state after receiving one of the first recorded divorces in California.

Financial setbacks, family deaths, and the difficulty of running a ranch eventually pushed her back east in 1856, but not before she had left a vivid portrait of California's early years and a model of a woman claiming public authority in a place that barely recognized such a thing.

Medicine, Asylums, and War

Back in New York, she continued her medical studies and pursued writing and lecturing. In 1857, she founded the Women's Protective Emigration Society and helped relocate unemployed women to Illinois and Indiana in search of work. By the late 1850s, Eliza turned to the new frontiers of reform. She studied medicine informally, then returned west in 1859 to serve as matron of the female department at the Stockton Insane Asylum in California, where she again pushed for more humane conditions. Her experiences there deepened her critique of how institutions treated those who did not fit social norms, especially women.

In the early 1860s, she came back east for the last time, now writing and lecturing on abolition, women's rights, and what she framed as the "era" of women's moral leadership. During the Civil War, she served as a volunteer nurse among the wounded at Gettysburg in 1863, working in makeshift hospitals crowded with broken bodies from both sides of the conflict.

September 6, 1862, Harper's Weekly, "The Influence of Women," Library of Congress

At that time, battlefield medicine was crude, overwhelmed, and often indistinguishable from organized suffering. Nurses worked in airless ward tents or hastily converted warehouses where the smell of blood, burned flesh, chloroform, and gangrene clung to every surface. Amputations were performed in rows, sometimes a dozen or more before the same surgeon washed his hands; piles of severed limbs grew outside the operating flap.

Water was scarce, sanitation inconsistent, and lice, dysentery, and hospital gangrene spread faster than doctors could contain them. Nurses hauled buckets of ice, boiled dressings, lifted wounded men whose bodies were shattered by Minié balls, and tried to soothe fevered soldiers crying for morphine that had run out. Nights were the worst—kerosene lamps casting long shadows over men drifting in and out of consciousness while wagons unloaded new casualties until dawn. This was the world Farnham stepped into: relentless labor, primitive conditions, and the constant knowledge that her patients survived not because the system was adequate, but because individuals like her refused to look away.

The ordeal and strain of this experience likely worsened a case of tuberculosis she had already contracted.[3]

Eliza Farnham died in New York City on December 15, 1864, at forty-nine. She was buried in the Friends' (Quaker) Cemetery at Milton-on-Hudson, a quietly radical woman laid to rest in ground associated with another long tradition of reform.

A Frontier of Institutions

Eliza Farnham never carried a gun into battle or smuggled fugitives across a river. Her frontiers were institutional: a women's cell block, a Gold Rush ranch, an asylum ward, a battlefield tent. In each, she tested how far a woman could push against accepted uses of power—replacing silence with speech at Sing Sing, insisting that California's promise be measured by the lives of its women and children, demanding that even the mad and the wounded be treated as capable of some dignity and change.

144

Where Susanna Dickinson's courage was forged in a single day of war, and Delia Webster's in an open act of civil disobedience, Eliza Farnham's lay in years of slow, grinding conflict with the everyday machinery of punishment and profit—arguing, on the eastern seaboard and the far western coast alike, that any civilization worthy of the name had to prove itself in how it treated the women and the powerless at its edges.

Illustration, Eliza Farnham

[1] Levy, Joann. Unsettling the West: Eliza Farnham and Georgiana Bruce Kirby in Frontier California. Santa Clara University: California Legacy Series, 2004.

[2] Bakken, G., & Farrington, B. (2003). Encyclopedia of Women in the American West, p. 124. Thousand Oaks: Sage.

[3] Atwater, Edward C (2016). Women Medical Doctors in the United States before the Civil War: A Biographical Dictionary. Rochester, NY: University of Rochester Press.

Chapter 13 — Clara Brown: Angel of the Rockies and Builder of Colorado's Black Community

"I always go where Jesus calls me."

— Clara Brown

CLARA BROWN WALKED INTO Colorado history carrying very little that the world valued—no money, no paperwork to prove an education, only the scars of slavery and the memory of four children sold away from her in Kentucky. Yet by the time she died in 1885, this formerly enslaved laundress had become "Aunt Clara," one of the best-known women in the Rockies: a successful investor, a founding member of local churches, and, most of all, the quiet force behind a new Black community in the mining towns of the high country.

Sold Apart, Walking West

Clara was born enslaved in Virginia around 1800 and moved as a child with her owner's household to Logan County, Kentucky. At eighteen, she married another enslaved person, Richard Brown; together they had four children—Richard, Margaret, Paulina Ann, and Eliza Jane—living under the constant threat that any one of them could be sold at a moment's notice.

That fear became reality in the mid-1830s. When their owner, Ambrose Smith, died around 1835, his human property was liquidated. Clara's husband and all four of her children were sold to different buyers in different locations; she never saw three of them again. The sale left her alone in Kentucky, still enslaved, with nothing left of her family but names and a determination she would carry for the rest of her life: to find them if she ever gained her freedom.

Freedom did not come quickly. She passed through the hands of several owners, working in households and fields. Not until she was about fifty-six—sometime in the late 1850s—that her third owner in Kentucky freed her in his will, with the added legal condition that, as a formerly enslaved person, she had to leave the state. With no husband, no children, and no place to go, she fixed on a single distant possibility: there were rumors that one of her daughters, Eliza Jane, had been taken somewhere "out West."

Clara decided to head west and find her. She first worked as a cook and maid for a white family headed for Leavenworth, Kansas Territory. Later, she persuaded a group of gold prospectors to take her along on their wagon train as a cook in exchange for transportation and room for her heavy laundry kettles. In April 1859, with Colonel Benjamin Wadsworth's outfit, she began the tough eight-week journey across the plains to the Colorado goldfields. At least one white southerner in the group openly complained about "a black woman" traveling with them, but Clara endured the insults and kept cooking.[1]

By summer, she reached Cherry Creek, the twin frontier settlements of Denver and Auraria, and then followed the stream of hopeful men up into the mountains toward a scatter of new mining camps. She was fifty-nine years old, with no family and not a dollar in savings—but she had reached the place where she meant to start again.

Denver, 1859, Collier & Cleveland Litho Co. - Library of Congress Prints and Photographs Division Washington, D.C. 20540 http://hdl.loc.gov/loc.pnp/cph.3b49610, Public Domain, https://commons.wikimedia.org/w/index.php?curid=1648024

Laundress of Central City

Clara settled in the booming camp then called Mountain City, soon absorbed into Central City in Gilpin County, the heart of Colorado's hard-rock gold rush. There, tens of thousands of young men dug, hammered, and blasted in claims that left them filthy, exhausted, and often sick. They needed clean clothes, warm meals, and someone to patch them up when they fell ill or were injured.

She opened what is widely described as the first commercial laundry in Central City, hauling water, boiling clothes in her big kettles, and charging prices that seem modest today but added up in a town where miners constantly cycled through shirts and trousers covered in sweat and ore dust. She also cooked meals and offered her services as a midwife and nurse, caring for sick and injured men who sometimes had no one else to look after them.

This wasn't just neighborly kindness—it was survival strategy. Clara understood something crucial: in an environment this harsh, cooperation wasn't optional; it created informal but highly effective networks for medical care, education, and emotional sustenance. By providing help in an isolating landscape, these networks became the foundation of prairie communities. Before there were churches, schools, or town halls, there were women like Clara visiting each other, sharing resources, and building the social infrastructure that would eventually become towns.

Clara lived frugally, sleeping in a simple cabin and spending little on herself. By the end of the Civil War, she had saved thousands of dollars. Contemporary sources put her holdings at around $10,000 by 1866, an enormous sum for the era and particularly remarkable for a woman who, only a decade earlier, had been enslaved. She was among the few who realized that, in a camp economy, the surest money wasn't always in the mines; it was in real estate, services, and, eventually, in carefully chosen claims.[2]

She bought lots in Central City and nearby towns, some of them in growing commercial districts, and took small stakes in local mining ventures. Not every investment paid off, and fires destroyed some of her properties, but over time, she became one of the more prosperous residents of Gilpin County.

Her cabin, however, never became a fortress of wealth. Neighbors remembered that her door was always open to anyone in need. People began to call her "Aunt Clara," and one admirer later wrote that her modest home served as "a hospital, a home, a general refuge for those who were sick or in poverty." She hosted the first Methodist services in Central City at her house and contributed her time and money to at least four different congregations, including Catholic and Protestant churches, long before church buildings were established.

The Angel of the Rockies

When the Civil War ended, and emancipation turned millions of enslaved people into citizens without land or resources, Clara saw in their faces the position she herself had been in years before. Around 1866, with her laundry and property still generating income, she took the first steps in a new mission: bringing other Black families west.

She returned to Kentucky and Tennessee, visiting the counties where she had once lived, and used her savings to pay passage for formerly enslaved men, women, and children to travel by rail and wagon to Colorado. Credible estimates say she personally financed journeys for at least 16 people and, over time, as many as two dozen. She did not simply drop them at the depot; she helped them find housing and jobs in Central City and Denver, effectively seeding one of the first stable Black communities in the territory.

Her charity went beyond relocation. She regularly took in sick or injured miners at her own expense, feeding and nursing them back to health. She gave generously to church building funds, contributing to the first Protestant church in the Rockies and supporting Catholic and Methodist congregations alike. She also helped fund education: at least one source notes that she provided scholarships for young Black women to attend Oberlin College in Ohio, an institution famous for training Black teachers and activists.

Her reputation spread beyond Colorado. In 1879, when large numbers of Black "Exoduster" migrants flooded into Kansas seeking land and safety, the governor of Colorado sent Clara—then nearly eighty—to Kansas to see how best Colorado charities could support them and to encourage some to consider resettling in the mountains. She moved through refugee camps and new Black farming communities, listening and carrying information back across the plains.

Yet through all of this, one search never left her: she still hoped to find her lost daughter, Eliza Jane. She spent thousands of dollars on advertisements, rewards, and travel, offering as much as $10,000 for news of Eliza Jane's whereabouts. For decades, nothing came.

Reunion and Farewell

In 1882, she finally received word that Eliza Jane had been found in Council Bluffs, Iowa. The daughter, now in her fifties and widowed, had believed her mother to be long dead. In 1884, Clara went to Iowa to reunite with Eliza Jane and meet a granddaughter she had never known. They spent time together that year, filling in fifty years of absence with stories. After a lifetime of losses, Clara had finally found a single thread of her family again.

Clara Brown

That same year, 1884, the Society of Colorado Pioneers—an organization that honored those who had arrived in the territory before 1861—admitted her as its first female member and granted her a small stipend in recognition of "her lifetime of good works." It was a rare formal acknowledgment, by a society that had often marginalized women and people of color, that Clara Brown had been essential to building the place they now celebrated.

Clara died in Denver in 1885 at about eighty-five years old. Her funeral at Central Presbyterian Church attracted governors, mayors, and prominent citizens, who praised "Aunt Clara" as a pioneer and philanthropist. She was buried with honors from the Society of Colorado Pioneers. This organization had once been almost entirely white and male, but it now stopped to honor a formerly enslaved Black woman as one of Colorado's founding figures.

In the years since, Colorado has slowly caught up to that judgment. Her name appears in the Colorado Women's Hall of Fame, the Colorado Business Hall of Fame, and on exhibits from Central City's opera house to the state capitol. Nonprofits and housing projects in Denver now bear her name, holding up her life as a model of community-building across lines of race and class.

The numbers tell one story—tens of thousands of dollars earned, invested, and given away; at least sixteen lives carried west by her savings. But the deeper story is about a woman who had every reason to hoard whatever safety she could find, and instead spent her wealth and her old age opening doors for people who looked like the woman she had once been—just freed, alone, and standing on the edge of a new country, trying to decide whether it could also be home.

This statue of Clara Brown is on display at the National Museum of African American History and Culture in Washington, DC.

[1] Varnell, Jeanne (1999). Women of Consequence: The Colorado Women's Hall of Fame. Boulder: Johnson Press.
[2] Katz, W (1995). "Chapter 7. Clara Brown of Colorado". Black Women of the Old West. New York: Antheum Books for Young Readers, Simon and Schuster.

Closing Thoughts

"The land is our mother; it gives us everything we need."

—Buffalo Bird Woman (Waheenee), Hidatsa elder

The story of the American frontier cannot be told honestly without the women who built it, endured it, and remembered it. Their labor fed families and stabilized settlements; their decisions shaped communities; their memories preserved the truth beneath the myth. The frontier was not only a landscape of open sky and hardship—it was a lived environment in which women negotiated danger, loss, survival, and hope with a steadiness that has long gone under-recognized.

Across diaries, letters, oral histories, and government records, a shared pattern emerges. Whether emigrant or Indigenous, wealthy or destitute, missionary or homesteader, women confronted the consequences of westward expansion more intimately than most men. They managed households on the move, gave birth in isolation, buried children along wagon roads, rebuilt homes after raids or removals, mediated cultural conflict, and found moments of resilience amid scarcity. Many lived without the protection of law or the support of established communities. Yet they carved meaning, structure, and continuity into a world defined by instability.

For Native women, the frontier era brought upheaval, forced displacement, and the erosion of ancestral homelands. Their stories reveal a different perspective— one of protection, negotiation, cultural endurance, and ongoing resistance to policies that reshaped entire nations. Their experiences are not parallel to those of emigrant women but intertwined with them, illuminating a broader, more complete account of what the frontier truly was.

The women whose stories appear in these pages did not live for glory or legacy. Most never imagined their writing would become a historical record. But they left a trail nonetheless: ink on paper, memories held within families, and oral traditions that withstood generations of change. Through them, we gain a clearer view of a past too often flattened into legend.

Their courage was not always dramatic. It was daily. Repetitive. Uncelebrated. It lived in the simple act of enduring another storm, another illness, another mile, another season. And that quiet perseverance shaped the American West as much as any treaty, battle, or railroad.

Their stories are not footnotes to a larger tale. They are the story.

Acknowledgements

This book would not exist without the women whose voices, memories, and lives shaped the history of the American frontier. Their diaries, letters, oral traditions, and testimonies form the backbone of this work, and I am grateful to every archivist, historian, and family descendant who preserved their records so they could be heard today.

My thanks go to the librarians, curators, and staff at numerous institutions whose collections provided the primary sources that grounded this narrative, including the Oregon Historical Society, the National Archives, the Bancroft Library, the Kansas Historical Society, and regional tribal cultural centers that safeguard community histories. Their meticulous stewardship of historical materials ensures that the truth of the frontier endures.

I am deeply indebted to scholars of women's history, Native American studies, and western expansion whose research has illuminated pathways through a complex and often mythologized past. Their commitment to rigorous, evidence-based interpretation made this work possible.

To the communities and descendants who continue to protect and interpret their ancestral histories—thank you for your generosity, knowledge, and persistence in keeping these stories alive.

My appreciation also extends to the early readers and researchers who offered thoughtful feedback, identified errors, and helped refine the narrative so that it remained both accurate and accessible.

Finally, I am grateful to those who encouraged this project from its earliest concept through its final pages. Your support, questions, and insistence on truth over myth sustained the work at every stage.

Notes on Sources

This book draws on a broad range of historical materials to present a clear, well-supported account of women's lives on the American frontier. The record is uneven—rich in emigrant diaries and letters, thinner in surviving firsthand accounts by Indigenous women—so the narrative relies on the strongest available documentation, supported by reliable modern scholarship.

Core Sources

The foundation of this book comes from firsthand accounts and contemporary records, including:

Women's diaries and letters from the Oregon, California, and Mormon Trails, preserved in collections such as Covered Wagon Women, Pioneer Girl, and archival holdings of institutions including the Oregon Historical Society, the Huntington Library, and regional historical societies.

Missionary and autobiographical writings by women such as Narcissa Whitman, Eliza Spalding, and Sarah Winnemucca, whose Life Among the Piutes remains one of the most important nineteenth-century narratives written by a Native American woman.

Contemporary newspapers, emigrant guides, military reports, and government documents that provide context for migration patterns, treaty negotiations, and demographic change.

Oral histories recorded in the late nineteenth and early twentieth centuries, particularly those preserving Native women's experiences, maintained through tribal historical programs and early ethnographic work.

These sources form the factual backbone of the narrative. Quotations are reproduced faithfully, with spelling or punctuation adjusted only when necessary for clarity.

Supporting Scholarship

Modern historical works are used to clarify chronology, verify details, and place individual lives within their broader historical setting. This includes scholarship on westward migration, Native American history, women's history, and material culture, as well as biographies that reconstruct frontier lives through archival research. These works help ensure that personal accounts are presented accurately and responsibly.

Interpreting a Fragmented Record

Where accounts differ—as they sometimes do between emigrant narratives and tribal oral histories—those differences are acknowledged rather than smoothed over. The aim is not to impose a single version of events, but to present a fuller picture of frontier life by placing women's voices from different communities side by side.

Documentation

Endnotes are provided for quotations, events, and factual claims so interested readers can follow the sources without interrupting the flow of the story. Anecdotes and quotations are included only when they can be traced to identifiable primary material or to well-established historical research.

Author's Note

The women in this book were real.

They cooked over open hearths, buried children, bartered for seed, argued with officials, stood up to husbands, mourned stolen homelands, and watched the map of North America redraw itself around them. Wherever possible, their stories are rooted in the words they left behind: diaries and letters, court records and newspaper accounts, agency reports, reminiscences told late in life. When those sources are silent or fragmentary—as they so often are for women, and especially for Native, Black, and poor women—I have leaned on the best available scholarship to fill in the larger historical frame.

This is a work of narrative history. That means I have tried to tell true stories in a way that reads like a story, not like a textbook. Timelines have been tightened, long journeys compressed, and occasionally I have moved a minor event forward or back in time when doing so does not change the known facts but makes the arc easier to follow. When I describe a landscape, a weather pattern, a tool, or a routine chore, those details come from period sources and material culture studies. Still, we do not always have a diarist saying, "On this exact day, I saw this exact scene." Think of those passages as historically grounded reconstructions rather than verbatim transcripts of a single moment.

I have not invented major characters, dramatic incidents, or outcomes. If a key event appears here—a battle, a massacre, a court case, a treaty council, a failed harvest—it is because there is documentation for it. When I quote directly from a diary, letter, or report, the quotation is faithful to the original, including its spelling and punctuation, unless otherwise noted. In a few places, I have gently modernized spelling or grammar in the main text for readability; fuller, unedited quotations can be found in the notes on sources.

Language is one of the most complex parts of writing about the nineteenth-century American West. Many of the documents we rely on were written by white observers who described Native people, Mexican and Mexican American communities, and Black neighbors in terms that are painful and racist. In the main narrative, I avoid those terms. In direct quotations, I have sometimes left the original language in place when it is vital for understanding the writer's attitude or the era's violence. When you see harsh words in quotation marks, they are there to show you what these women were up against, not to endorse the language.

Names can be equally complicated. A single woman might appear in the records under a baptismal name, a married name, a nickname, and, if she was Native, a name in her own language rendered in several different English spellings. In general, I have chosen the name most often used by historians today and noted alternatives in the back matter. For Native women whose nations still exist, I have tried to use tribal names and spellings that reflect current usage, while acknowledging what appears in the nineteenth-century sources.

Any time we follow women onto the American prairie, we also step into contested ground. For Indigenous women in particular, this was not "frontier" in the romantic sense; it

166

was home long before the first sod house was cut or the first wagon rolled through. Homesteaders' dreams became possible only because treaties were broken, lands were seized, and Native communities were pushed aside, confined, or killed. This book does not attempt to tell every side of every story, but it does not treat that violence as background scenery. When a woman's courage or "success" depended on systems that harmed others, I have tried to be honest about that.

Readers who work with primary sources will notice that some scenes feel closer and more detailed than others. That is not a reflection of whose lives were more important, but of whose lives were more thoroughly recorded—and whose papers were deemed worth preserving. A white homesteader who left three complete diaries may have a more straightforward, day-to-day narrative than a Native woman whose story must be reconstructed from government reports, missionary accounts, and the memories of descendants. The imbalance is in the archive, not in the women.

The notes on sources at the back of this book are there for several reasons. They show you where particular episodes and quotations came from. They point you toward historians, tribal historians, and community scholars who have been working on these stories far longer than I have. And they are a reminder that history is not owned; it is a conversation you are now invited into. If something in these pages sends you to an archive, a digital collection, a tribal cultural center, or a local historical society, then this book has done one of its most important jobs.

Despite careful research, any errors or oversights are mine alone. Geography is vast, records are incomplete, and perspectives differ. If you are a descendant, a community member, or a scholar who sees a detail that needs correction or a voice that should be added in future editions, I welcome that conversation.

Most of all, I hope you come away from these pages with a clearer sense that the "prairie" was never an empty backdrop and that the women who crossed it—or refused to leave it—were not supporting characters in someone else's story. They were decision-makers, interpreters, organizers, laborers, survivors, and sometimes resisters in their own right. Remembering them with as much accuracy and humility as we can is one small way of honoring that fact.

About the Author

Ward McLendon is a writer and analyst whose work explores the intersection of history and culture. A former public opinion analyst and message strategist, he has advised political campaigns, environmental organizations, CEOs, and philanthropic foundations on how ideas move people.

He is also the author of The Ghost Dance War and recently modernized the classic A History of Kansas, updating it from its original 1919 publication, which traces the state's past from frontier settlement to statehood.

A Request from the Author

If this book spoke to you or provided helpful context on the lives of women on the American Frontier, a short book review is appreciated.

Reviews keep nonfiction history accessible to future generations and are greatly appreciated by authors and independent publishers like us.

The full catalog of books by Ward McLendon and Unbound Press can be found at

www.unboundpressbooks.com

More books by Ward McLendon:

Ghost Dance War

(Coming soon)

Bleeding Kansas: A Reader's Companion

Early Topeka

Preview of the Ghost Dance War, by Ward McLendon

The following pages include a preview from The Ghost Dance War, available at bookstores and online at Amazon.com, Barnes and Noble, and <u>www.unboundpressbooks.com</u>

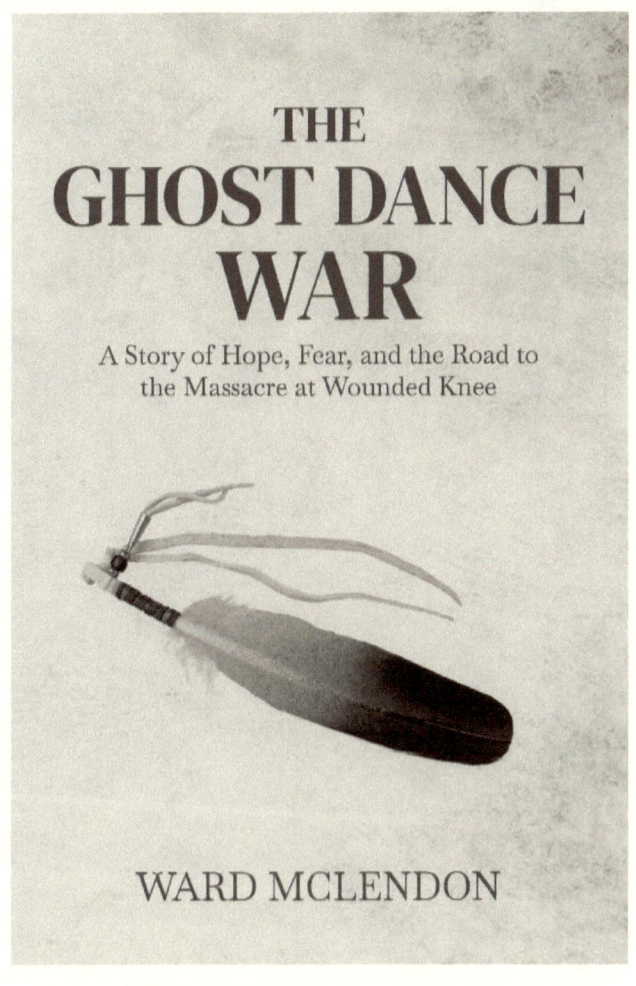

THE
GHOST DANCE WAR

A Story of Hope, Fear, and the Road to
the Massacre at Wounded Knee

WARD MCLENDON

Introduction

THE GHOST DANCE DID not begin as a rebellion. It began as a prayer.

It was delivered through visions and songs, driven by a desperate hope that the world could be restored after decades of loss. The loss of land, freedom, ceremony, and the right to live as a sovereign people. But within two years, that hope clashed with federal fear, military misjudgment, and a national desire to erase anything opposing the march of American expansion.

This book tells the story of that collision.

It traces the journey from its inception in Nevadan prophecy to its expansion across the Plains; from reservation hunger and broken treaties to Washington's panic over "uprisings" that never truly happened. It explores the political, military, tribal, and personal choices that tightened around the Lakota people like a noose. It also follows how misunderstanding turned into policy, policy into force, and force into the massacre at Wounded Knee.

This is not a retelling of Bury My Heart at Wounded Knee, but rather a focused reconstruction of the Ghost Dance era itself: the spiritual renewal, the increasing misinformation, the deadly choices, and the final moments that changed Native–U.S. relations for generations.

The aim is to show what happened, why it occurred, and how a movement rooted in peace became the pretext for the final major event of the Indian Wars.

If America wants to understand the cost of its westward triumph and the roots of its unresolved historical divides, it must understand the Ghost Dance War.

Chapter 1 — The World Before: Life on the Great Plains and a Continent in Collapse

"The American Indian is of the soil, whether it be the region of forests, plains, pueblos, or mesas. He fits into the landscape, for the hand that fashioned the continent also fashioned the man for his surroundings. He once grew as naturally as the wild sunflowers; he belongs just as the buffalo belonged."

– Luther Standing Bear, Oglala Sioux Chief

A World Unraveled

THE GREAT PLAINS, KNOWN for its vast, flat terrain, is an expanse of grasslands in central North America, stretching from the Rocky Mountains to the Missouri River. Once primarily grazing territory for wild buffalo and home to many nomadic Native American tribes, by 1890, it was overrun by adventurers, hopeful pioneers, miners, and missionaries.

By that time, the opening of the American West had been unfolding for nearly 100 years.

It started in 1803 with the Louisiana Purchase, which doubled the size of the United States and included vast territories west of the Mississippi River. President Thomas

Jefferson negotiated the purchase of what was then known as the Louisiana Territory from France, adding 828,000 square miles to the U.S. and significantly fueling westward expansion.

In the years following the Louisiana Purchase, the United States still knew very little about the vast lands it had acquired on paper. To remedy this, President Jefferson commissioned the Lewis and Clark Corps of Discovery to explore the new territory; an expedition meant not only to map rivers and mountains but also to establish contact with the Native nations already living there.

The Corps' journals describe dozens of first encounters: diplomatic councils held along riverbanks, exchanges of gifts and food, efforts to establish trade, and cautious introductions between worlds that had never met on equal footing. Lewis and Clark arrived with instructions to present the United States as the new sovereign power, yet most tribes viewed the expedition as just another group of travelers passing through their homelands.

The expedition's notes showcase the vast diversity of Native societies across the West. They documented established trade routes, intertribal alliances, complex political structures, thriving economies, and legal and ceremonial systems that predate the United States. Many communities were flourishing, mobile, and, despite disruptions from earlier European contact, still deeply connected to their traditional ways.

But the Corps of Discovery was also a hinge moment.

It marked the first sustained encounter between the U.S. federal government and the Western tribes, and, in retrospect, the start of a century-long clash. The expedition's maps opened the West to American settlement; its reports fueled land speculation; its diplomatic overtures signaled future claims of authority. What Lewis and Clark saw as exploration, later policymakers regarded as justification.

The West was no longer an unfamiliar land. It was a territory the United States now intended to occupy.

Westward Push

During the 1840s and 1850s, the idea of "Manifest Destiny" drove further expansion, with key events such as the annexation of Texas in 1845, the Oregon Treaty of 1846, and the Mexican Cession in 1848, which added vast lands in the Southwest. Waves of settlers, miners, railroad workers, ranchers, and homesteaders moved west as the government promoted free land. Described as "unused" and available, federal land grants supported railroad construction, and the Homestead Act opened millions of acres for pioneer claims.

Across the plains, this change arrived in waves. Wagon by wagon, ranch by ranch, mining camp by mining camp. As pioneers pushed westward, the United States turned Native homelands into barriers to clear or control. When settlers moved further into Indigenous lands, the government responded not by halting the expansion but by restructuring Native nations, removing communities, redrawing boundaries, and deploying troops to secure the new frontier for American migration.

The Homestead Act of 1862 further encouraged settlers to claim land in areas the Lakota and other Plains tribes had relied on for generations. Each wagon trail crossing the plains undermined tribal sovereignty. Every new mining camp brought another intrusion. As pioneers moved westward, federal policies shifted to support the influx of settlers rather than those already living there.

By the 1870s and 1880s, U.S. policy had aligned around a single goal: to dismantle Native American independence and foster dependency. Resistance by tribes was met with military enforcement. Buffalo herds, once numbering in the tens of millions, were deliberately and systematically slaughtered to clear land for railroads and ranches. Federal Indian agents managed food distribution, withheld supplies as punishment, and enforced a new political order. The change was not just territorial; it marked a shift from sovereignty to surveillance, from nation to ward.

By 1887, mining, industrial expansion, and large-scale migration were reshaping the land, with cities and towns sprouting across the landscape and the rush for land and resources continuing strong. Railroad development cut through migration routes and hunting grounds.

The West was no longer a frontier of the past but a dynamic, rapidly changing part of the nation.

In this churn of movement and ambition, the Lakota stood at the center of the storm. To them, and other native inhabitants of the West, it seemed that a way of life that had lasted for generations was ending.

The Dawes Act

The Dawes Act of 1887, also known as the General Allotment Act, was a U.S. law that allowed the federal government to divide tribal lands into individual plots to encourage assimilation. It divided tribal communal land and assigned 160 acres to each Native American family, in the mistaken hope that they would become farmers.

It resulted in the loss of over 90 million acres of native land.

The goal, of course, was to assimilate Native Americans by ending their communal land ownership and encouraging them to adopt private property and farming, believing this would "civilize" them. What they truly wanted was for them to disappear. By breaking up the tribal structure of the indigenous nations, the government was sending a message: You're no longer part of a tribe; you are individual landowners; you are Americans.

Only those Native Americans who accepted individual allotments were granted U.S. citizenship. The remaining "surplus" tribal lands were then sold to non-Native settlers and corporations.

The Dawes Act, a well-meaning effort to help Indians, ended up hurting them instead. By 1890, no Indian people lived freely on their own land.

The Lakota

Before this expansion, the Lakota occupied one of the largest Indigenous territories in North America. Their land extended from the western banks of the Missouri River to the Powder River area in what is now Wyoming and Montana, and south into the Sandhills and Niobrara region of Nebraska. This landscape was not empty; it was full of meaning, memory, and movement.

The Lakota were one of the three main divisions of the Sioux Nation, along with Dakota and Nakota, forming the westernmost and most mobile branch. They had called the Plains home for over a century, and the sacred center of their world was the Black Hills (Pahá Sápa).

The Lakota were not simply residents of the land; they were its stewards. Over generations, they developed a network of trade, diplomacy, and seasonal migrations that connected them deeply to the rhythms of rivers, plains, and the sacred Black Hills. They were neither isolated nor static. Their influence stretched through alliances with tribes like the Cheyenne and Arapaho and through conflicts with the Crow, Pawnee, and others. They were a nation in the truest sense: sovereign, adaptable, interconnected, and mobile.

By the early 19th century, they had expanded westward after gaining horses and firearms and developing a culture well-suited to the grasslands.

Lakota society was organized around extended families, or tiyospaye, which formed the core of social and political life. Decisions were made through consensus, not command; leaders earned influence through generosity, skill, and moral authority rather than inherited or coercive power. The political structure was decentralized yet cohesive, allowing bands to act independently but unite against common threats.

White explorers who encountered them in the 1830s and 1840s repeatedly remarked on their population, their political cohesion, and the strength of their military organization. These were not fragmented or vulnerable people. This was a nation at its height.

Their society was finely adapted to the world around them: mobile, resilient, bound by kin groups, and organized through a decentralized but cohesive political structure.

They maintained extensive trade networks stretching from the Upper Mississippi to the foothills of the Rockies; governed themselves through a combination of band councils, respected leaders, and consensus decision-making; and upheld a social order that balanced personal freedom with communal responsibility.

Their life revolved around mobility, seasonal migration, and the buffalo, which provided food, clothing, shelter, tools, and spiritual grounding. To the Lakota, the land was not a possession but a living system: one they belonged to, moved through, and protected.

Their mobility was strategic, not improvised: the seasonal hunting routes, winter camps along sheltered river valleys, and intertribal diplomacy that managed alliances, marriages, and conflicts across a broad area created a stable political and cultural system. This system was adaptable enough to shift with the seasons while remaining strong enough to maintain unity among the people.

Spiritually, the Lakota saw the world as animated by interconnected forces, with wakan, the sacred power that flowed through everything at its center. Ceremonies such as the Sun Dance, sweat lodge, and vision quests tied individuals to the community and the cosmos. Their culture had resilience and balance precisely because it was oriented toward relational, not hierarchical, principles. These vision quests and ceremonies were not peripheral to life; they were integral to how the Lakota were bonded to one another, to the land, and to their ancestors.

This was the world that collided with U.S. expansion. A society built on mobility confronted a policy built on confinement. A political order grounded in consensus met a federal system that insisted on singular, enforceable authority. A people whose identity was rooted in the land found themselves pushed off it, parcel by parcel.

The Buffalo

The buffalo, which had been central to the economic, spiritual, and social life of Plains nations for decades, was the first great foundation to fall. In the early 1800s, tens of millions roamed the Plains. By 1889, fewer than a thousand remained in the wild.

The loss was fueled by commercial hide-hunting industries that exploded after 1870, fueled by new tanning technologies, aggressive railroad promotions, and a tacit military belief that buffalo eradication would force Native populations into dependency. Without the buffalo, tribal autonomy collapsed.

The Spark at Bozeman

The tension between tribes and the U.S. government grew worse in the 1860s when the Army opened the Bozeman Trail, a shortcut heading north into the Montana goldfields that cut straight through hunting grounds guaranteed to the Lakota by the 1851 treaty. The Powder River country, home to some of the last great buffalo herds, was not just a resource base; it was a cultural heartland, a place where generations of Lakota hunted, fought, negotiated, and prayed.

Red Cloud, a prominent Oglala war chief, immediately realized that the trail threatened not just mobility but their very survival. The Army started building forts to guard the road, and Red Cloud viewed each fort as a blow to Lakota sovereignty.

He responded with resistance rather than with diplomacy.

Between 1866 and 1868, Red Cloud led a coalition of Lakota, Cheyenne, and Arapaho warriors in what became known as Red Cloud's War. Through strategic ambushes, raids, and a deep understanding of the terrain, he achieved something rare in U.S.-Native conflict history: he forced the United States Army to retreat.

In 1868, the U.S. abandoned the forts and closed the Bozeman Trail. The victory was complete, but the repercussions would endure.

Fort Laramie and the Shifting Promises of a Nation

By the time Ulysses S. Grant took office in 1869, the United States was facing increasing conflicts with Native Americans across the West.

Grant's "Peace Policy," which aimed to reduce frontier violence and corruption, delegated control of many reservations to Christian denominations. Agents appointed under this system were often chosen based on religious ties rather than cultural understanding. They pushed for rapid assimilation, promoted English-only schools, banned ceremonies, and tried to restructure Native governance.

The paternalism of this policy sharply conflicted with the Lakota's political worldview. Leaders like Red Cloud, Spotted Tail, and Crazy Horse were used to negotiating from positions of strength. Now they had to contend with civilian agents who neither understood nor respected Lakota authority.

Tensions grew. Accusations of ration withholding, disrespect, and coercion became common. Several agents worked honestly and with some sympathy, but many others viewed Lakota culture as a problem to be corrected.

For the Lakota, the Peace Policy felt very much like a war on their identity. It attempted to remake them without their consent.

And it prepared the ground for conflicts that would erupt in the mid-1870s.

Among the most important agreements between the Lakota and the U.S. government was the 1868 Fort Laramie Treaty, signed after years of fighting along the Bozeman Trail. It granted the Lakota ownership of the Black Hills (Pahá Sápa) and a large territory set aside for their use. It also assured hunting rights, schools, rations, agency buildings, and protection from the Army against settlers moving in. For a time, it seemed to provide a stable peace.

That illusion lasted less than a decade.

Gold, Greed and the Theft of the Black Hills (Pahá Sápa)

In 1874, Lt. Col. George Armstrong Custer led an expedition into the Black Hills to confirm rumors of gold. His announcement triggered an invasion of miners, prospectors, and speculators. Thousands of people flooded into the treaty-protected area, and the federal government proved unwilling to remove them. Instead of honoring the treaty it had signed, Ulysses S. Grant shifted the government's position from protector to claimant. By 1877, Congress seized the Black Hills, taking away the Lakota's most sacred land in direct violation of the treaty's terms.

While the act was declared illegal more than a century later, it was irreversible for the people who lived through it.

The seizure of the Black Hills sparked a chain reaction that led to the Great Sioux War of 1876–77.

The most famous clash, the Battle of the Little Bighorn, resulted in one of the U.S. Army's most decisive defeats— and the death of George Armstrong Custer. But the victory was short-lived. The Army responded with overwhelming force. Winter campaigns, scorched-earth tactics, and

186

relentless pursuit ultimately forced many Lakota bands to surrender.

Crazy Horse was killed in 1877 under disputed circumstances. Others, like Sitting Bull, fled to Canada. The era of open conflict came to a close.

But the cost was immense: The buffalo were almost gone. Mobility was destroyed. Reservation boundaries were shrinking, and Federal oversight deepened.

The Lakota had survived the war, but the war had changed everything.

Now, the conflict shifted from the battlefield to the agency office. From military strategy to administrative policy. From open combat to what Lakota elders called "the slow killing."

Confined and Controlled: Early Reservation Life

As the land promised to the Lakota in 1868 began to fracture, the reservations that appeared afterward weren't safe homelands but isolated enclaves of confinement surrounded by an ever-expanding frontier.

Each new "agreement," often achieved through coercion or deception, eroded more land. Land that was once held collectively was divided into smaller plots; remaining acreage was opened for settlers; and reservations were repeatedly reduced to satisfy the increasing demands of railroads, ranchers, and homesteaders.

The authority shifted from tribal councils to federal agents, and the protected homelands promised in 1868 shrank into small, fenced enclaves of isolated pockets surrounded by a growing American frontier. The reservation system did more than restrict movement; it tore down the foundations of a functioning tribal nation.

One of the most devastating blows came in 1883, when the federal government issued the "Rules for Indian Courts," a set of regulations intended to control Native life. These rules criminalized many core religious practices, such as vision quests, and nearly all dances associated with community unity.

The punishments ranged from withholding rations to imprisonment within agency jails.

For the Lakota, whose spirituality was deeply woven into daily life, this ban was not just a minor administrative detail but an effort to uproot the very foundation of their world. Ceremonies served as moments when families mourned, healed, passed down knowledge, renewed alliances, and connected with ancestors. To outlaw them was to eliminate the mechanisms through which their society sustained itself.

Some ceremonies continued in secret, hidden from agents and missionaries. Others nearly disappeared.

Families who had lived self-sufficient lives for generations now depended on ration tickets, agency approval, and missionary oversight.

Boarding schools worsened the crisis. Native children were sent away for years, their hair cut, clothes replaced, languages punished, and religious customs forbidden. For many families, this forced separation was as heartbreaking as losing their land. The community's social core, its young people, was being molded through coercion.

Chiracahua Apache children arrive at the Carlisle Indian School, which was considered the model for many Native American boarding schools around the country. (National Archives, Records of the Office of the Chief Signal Officer)

At their core, these reservations were intended not as sanctuaries but as tools of control. They immobilized the tribes, severed them from their hunting grounds, and made their survival dependent on federal rations. By restricting movement, banning traditional governance, and policing cultural practices, the system sought to break down tribal identity from within. Indigenous families were moved, then moved again. Hunger became widespread. Federal agents replaced chiefs, schools replaced elders, and the rules of life were rewritten by men who had never lived on the land they claimed to govern.

The government expected the Lakota to become farmers, but the land was unsuitable for crops, and the tools provided were inadequate. Traditional governance structures were ignored or replaced. The Indian Police system enforced federal policies with increasing severity.

Christian missionaries banned ceremonies and destroyed sacred objects.

The spiritual world that had once been the core of Lakota identity now existed under surveillance. Elders watched sacred songs fall silent.

By the 1880s, reservation life could not compensate for what was lost. Lakota families were forced to line up for bags of flour, sugar, lard, and salt pork—items that bore no resemblance to their traditional diet and often caused illness. Malnutrition spread, and children suffered from chronic diseases that weakened their immune systems.

The world of the Plains tribes had unraveled so completely that it felt as if the ground itself had shifted beneath their feet. Generations of broken treaties, forced removals, confiscated lands, outlawed ceremonies, and the systematic dismantling of Native political life had left the Plains tribes feeling lost and dispossessed, struggling to survive on shrinking reservations that could no longer support their people.

The situation grew even more dire in 1889 when a severe drought hit, further decreasing crop yields and straining already scarce rations. Congressional budget cuts in 1890 lowered supplies to even more dangerous levels. Starvation was real; it was a daily struggle. In some Lakota families, adults gave up their portions so children could eat.

Within a single generation, nations that had once freely roamed across millions of acres, following the buffalo, holding ceremonies, and building complex alliances, found themselves confined to reservations governed by distant laws, indifferent bureaucracy, and a federal system that saw Indigenous cultures not as sovereign societies, but as problems to be solved.

Despair was common. But so was quiet resistance.

People kept languages alive in whispers. Ceremonies took place at night or deep in the hills. Stories were told to children who pretended not to understand English. By the late 1880s, a deep spiritual emptiness had settled over many Lakota communities.

This is the world into which the prophecy of renewal arrived.

A Message of Hope

The Standing Rock Reservation, situated on the border between North Dakota and South Dakota, is the home of the Standing Rock Sioux Tribe. It was there that the well-known Lakota medicine man Sitting Bull lived in his cabin.

In the fall of 1890, a Lakota named Kicking Bear visited him and brought remarkable news: a ceremony called the Ghost Dance was spreading among many tribes in the West. It was part of a message of hope for all Indian peoples delivered by a medicine man and prophet named Wovoka. If the people purified themselves and danced, the buffalo would once again cover the earth, and the white man would disappear.

"My brothers, I bring to you word from your fathers, the ghosts that they are marching now to join you. Led by the Messiah who came once to live on earth with the white man, but was killed by them. I bring to you the promise of a day in which there will be no more white man to lay his hand on the bridal of the Indian's horse and the Red men of the prairie will rule the world."

-        Kicking Bear

Sitting Bull was skeptical, but he agreed to let the dance be taught at Standing Rock.

As they mourned a life that seemed lost forever, they found comfort in the idea that maybe it was all just a bad dream.

www.unboundpressbooks.com